VATSALYA- A HOMEMADE SERIES FOR HOMESCHOOLING

PART I ENGLISH AGES 3+

NIDHI AGRAWAL

Copyright © Nidhi Agrawal
All Rights Reserved.

DEDICATED TO MY CHILDREN, VIHAAN AND VATSALYA.

THEY HAVE BEEN MY SOURCE OF INSIPRATION.

THE CHILDREN HAVE BEEN ABSOLUTELY PATIENT WITH ME WHILE I WAS ON MY JOURNEY TO CREATE THIS BOOK.

I ALSO WANT TO THANK MY BROTHER ANKIT AGRAWAL FOR CONSTANT SUPPORT AND ENCOURAGEMENT. MY HUSBAND WHO STOOD BY ME AGAINST ALL ODDS.

Contents

Preface

Covid phase has proved to be challenging to the educators specifically when the toddlers could not attend physical classes at all due to schools being closed. Pushing the small children to learn through online classes was even more challenging. Being a mother of three-year-old, I kept worrying about the right way to introduce English to my child who absolutely did not bother to listen to me. Home-schooling was therefore both necessary and challenging. I kept looking for the right book for my child but could not decide on which one to rely, since most of the books focused on picture presentation and tracing. This is when I finally decided to teach him English Alphabet through phonics. Within less than two months, I could see him saying the letters with ease, identify pictures and write neatly. All this could happen when he learnt the phonemes by heart. And now, he is a confident boy who can read words as well.

Therefore, to ease learning, I have developed a handmade home-schooling book, keeping in mind every minute detail and care that I took while educating my young one. The book contains phonetic sounds, pictures and writing assistance sheets for all the letters. Further, the letters have been segregated with respect to lines and curves so that the easy ones may be learnt first and then proceeding to the tough letters. The book also contains various practice sheets to assess the learning progress. In this Digital world where it is easy to copy and paste, creating a handmade book was a challenge which I took to make sure that the learning gained through educating my toddler is passed on to more and more mothers with personal love and care.

It is said that a stronger foundation paves way for a brighter future. I am sure that the book helps the educator to simplify the learning process and induce confidence in kids. And I am hopeful that even after covid ebbs, the book will continue to be useful to educators in teaching their children at home.

Good Luck!

CHAPTER ONE

INTRODUCTION

What is ENGLISH ?

English is a language.

English alphabet has 26 letters.

Each letter has a unique sound called phonics.

Learning letters through their phonetic sounds lasts in the minds of children forever.

LINES AND CURVES

LINES & CURVES
STANDING LINES
SLEEPING LINES
LEFT & RIGHT CURVES
BACKWARD & FORWARD SLANTING LINES
OPEN CURVES
COLOUR ME!
TRACE ME!

TRACE & COLOUR

3.

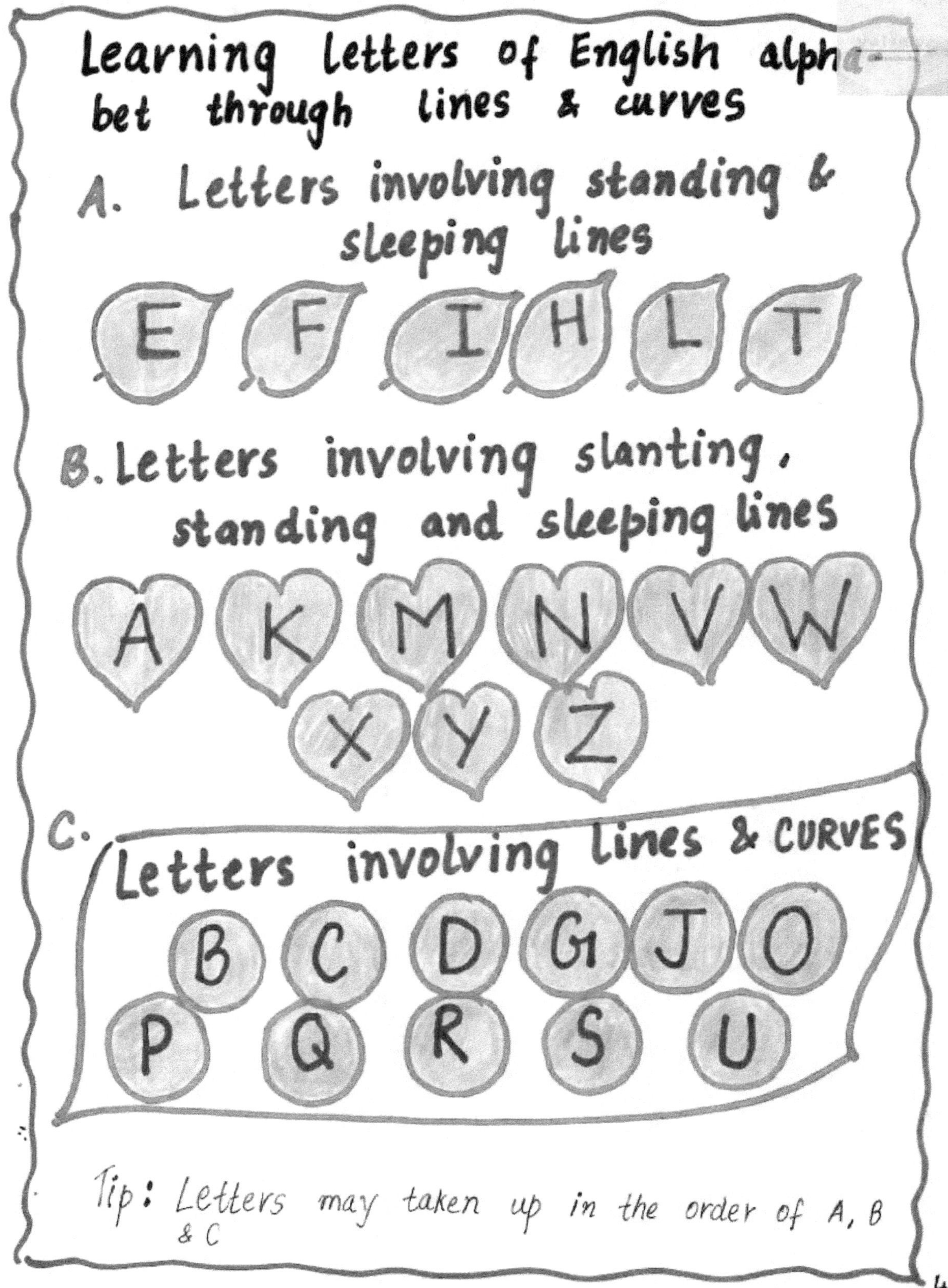
Learning letters of English alpha bet through lines & curves
A. Letters involving standing & sleeping lines
E F I H L T
B. Letters involving slanting, standing and sleeping lines
A K M N V W
X Y Z
C. Letters involving lines & CURVES
B C D G J O
P Q R S U
Tip: Letters may taken up in the order of A, B & C

4

LETTER Aa

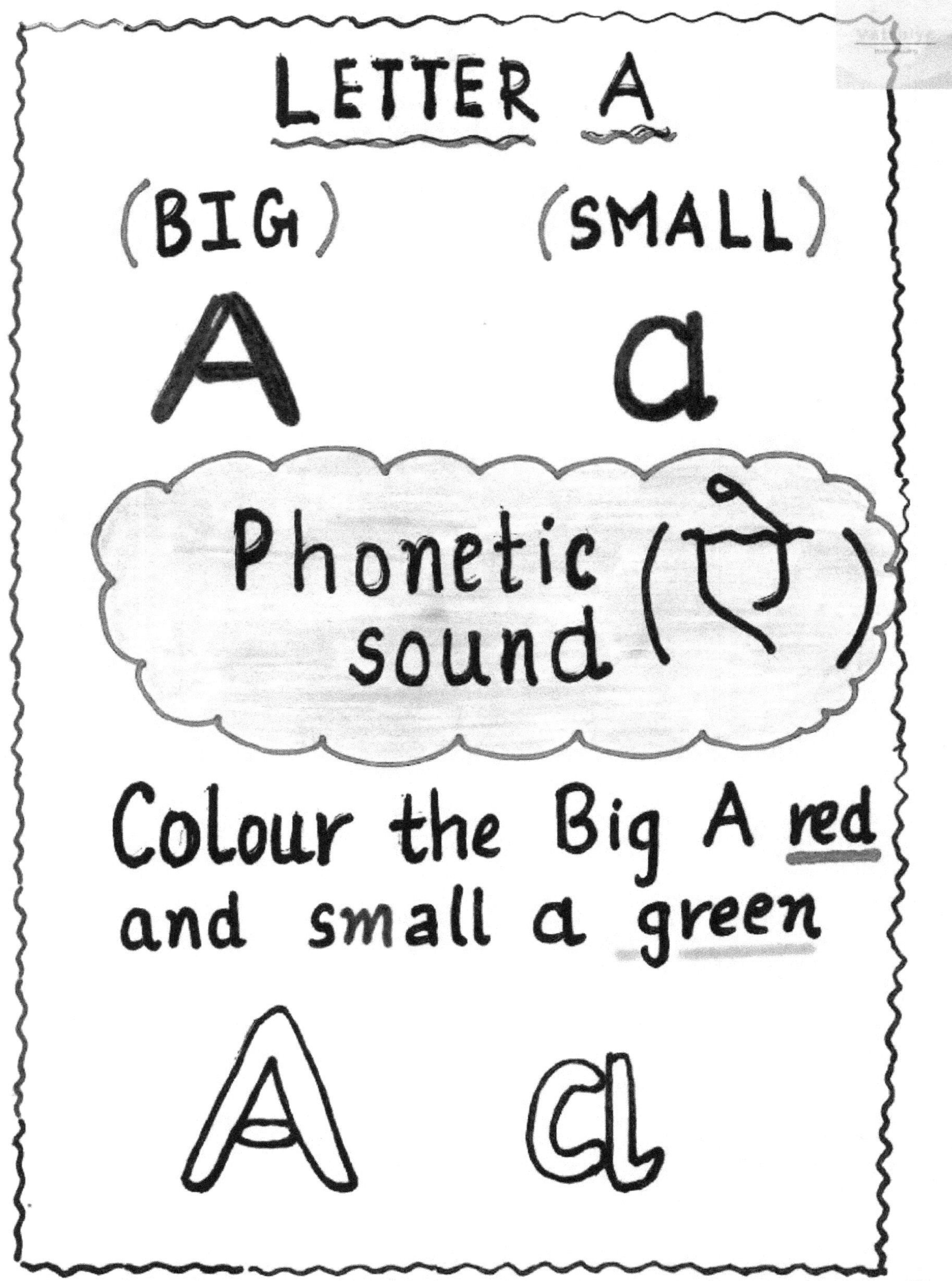

LETTER A
(BIG)
(SMALL)
A
a
Phonetic sound (ऐ)
Colour the Big A red
and small a green
A
a

5

Things with letter 'A'
Apple (ऐ)
(ऐ) Aeroplane
(ऐ) Arrow
(ऐ) Axe
(ऐ) Ant
(ऐ) Alligator
6

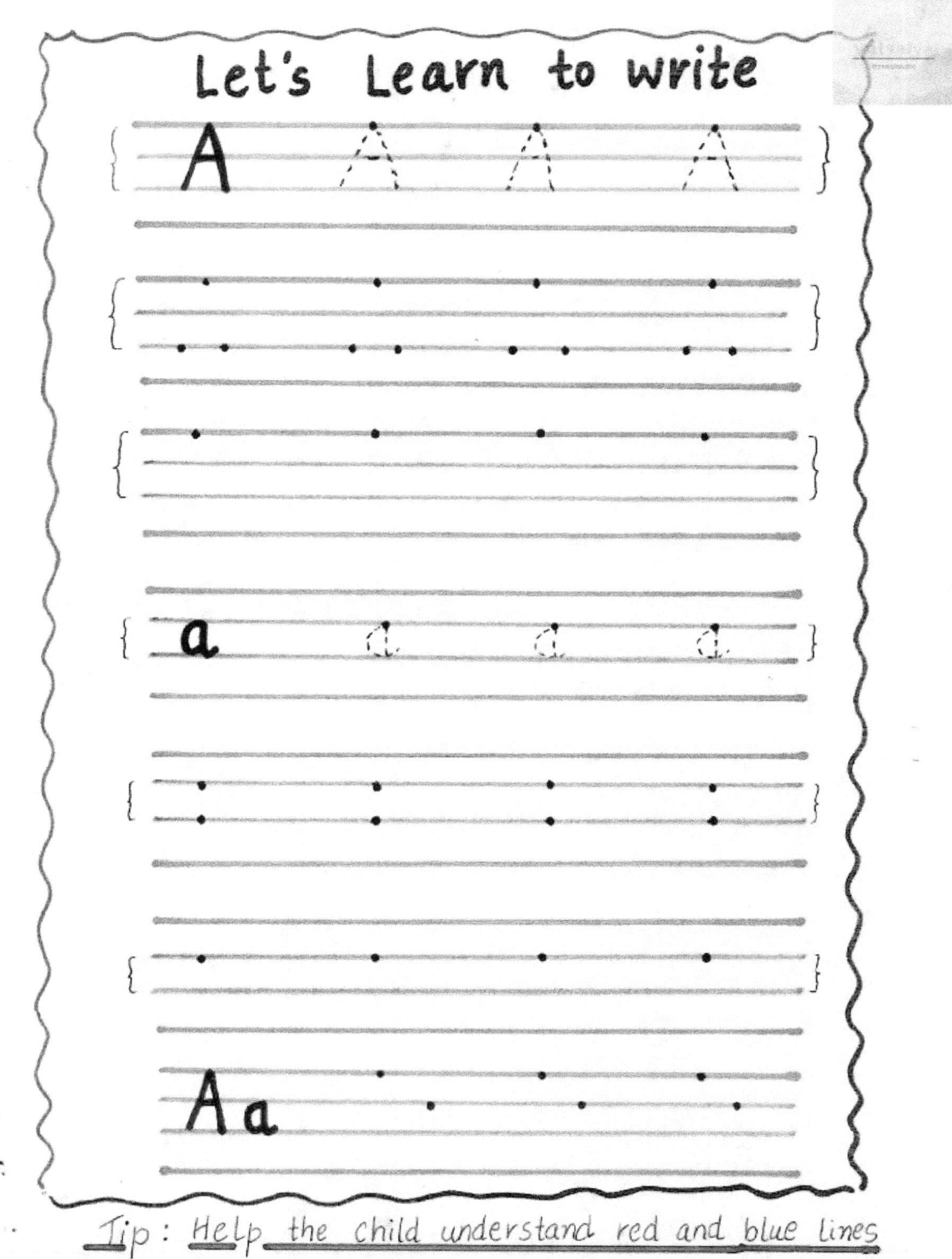

Tip: Help the child understand red and blue lines

7

LETTER Bb

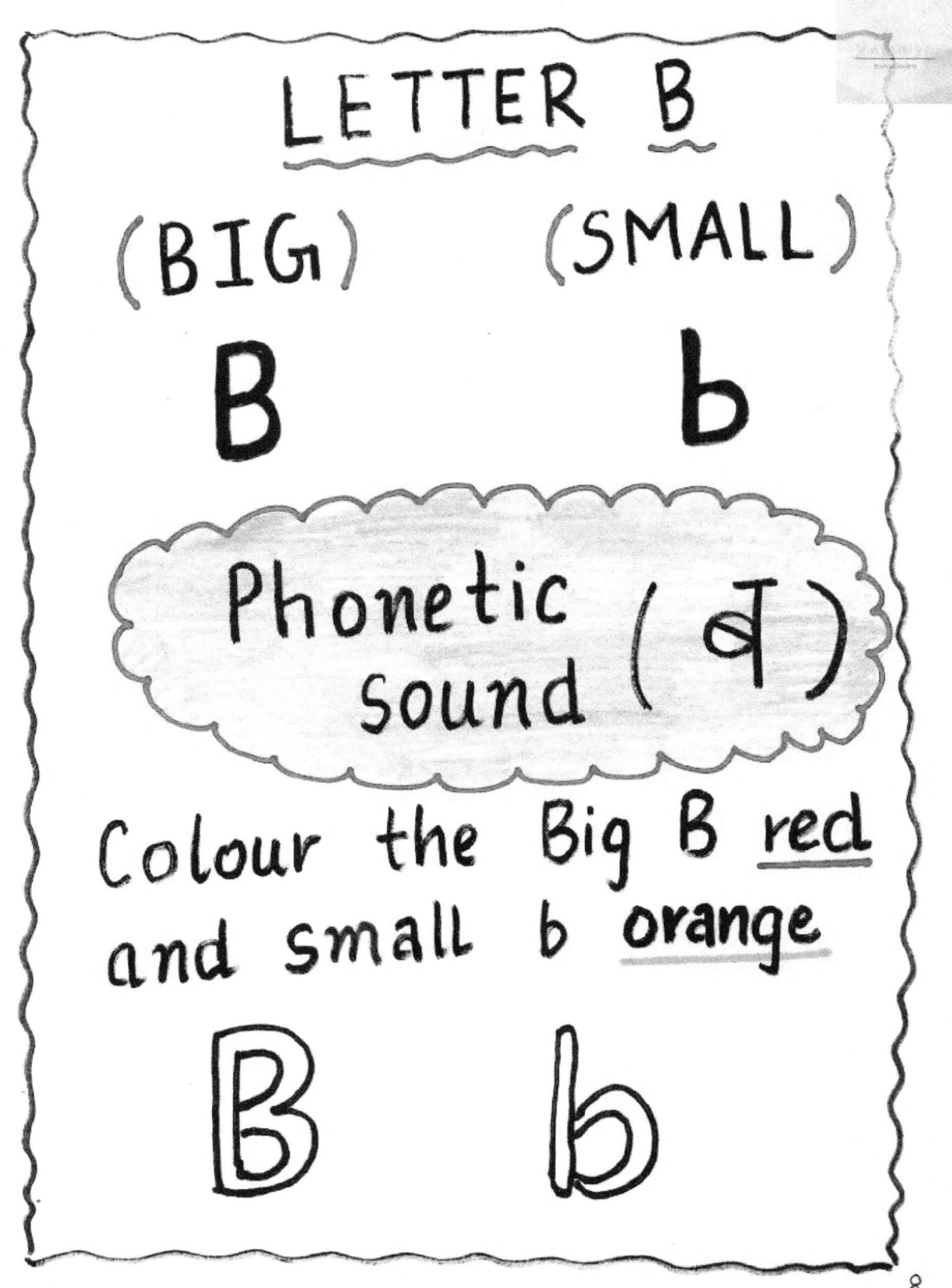

LETTER B
(BIG)   (SMALL)
B   b
Phonetic sound (ब)
Colour the Big B red
and small b orange
B   b

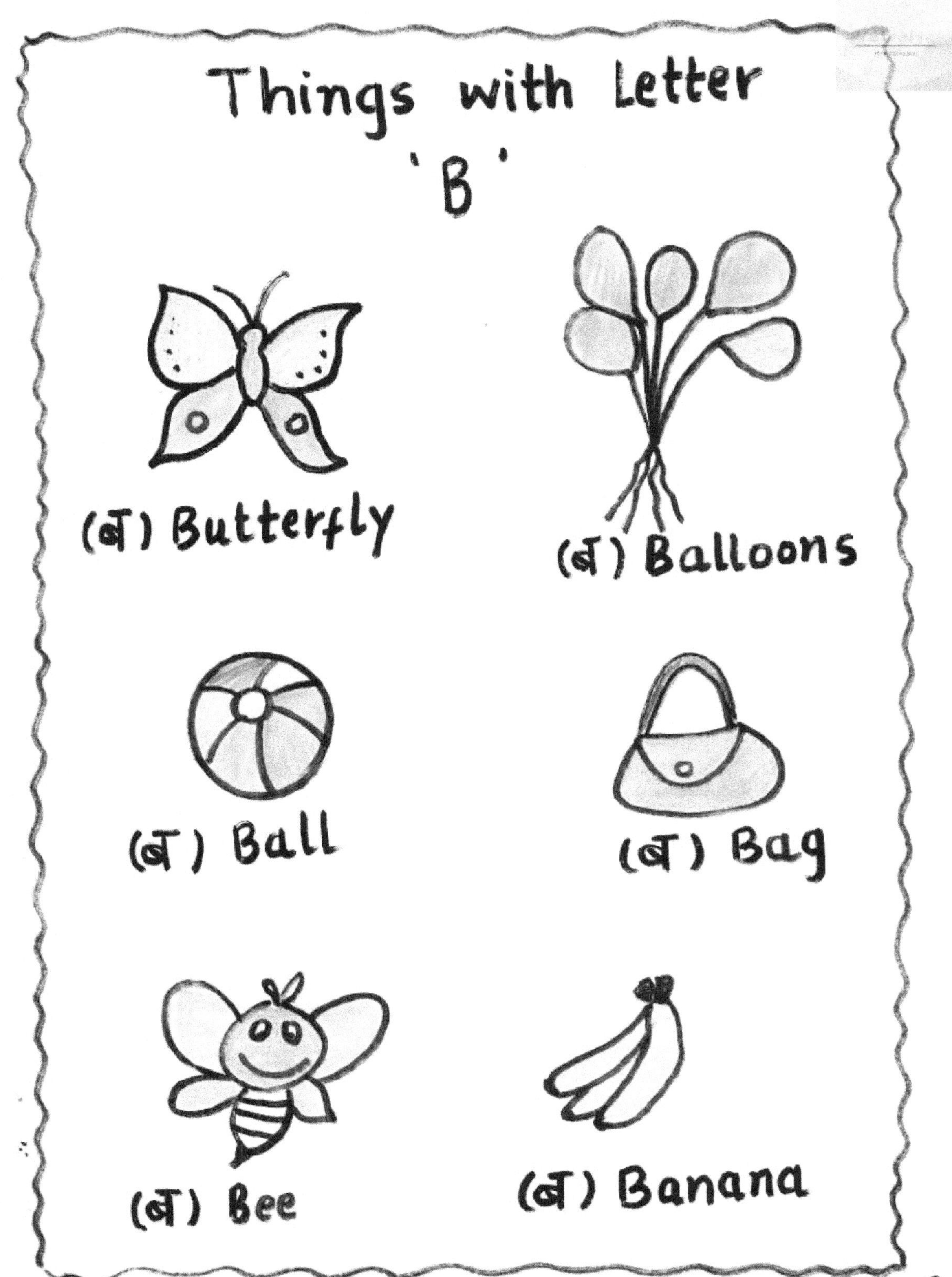

Things with Letter 'B'
(ब) Butterfly
(ब) Balloons
(ब) Ball
(ब) Bag
(ब) Bee
(ब) Banana
9

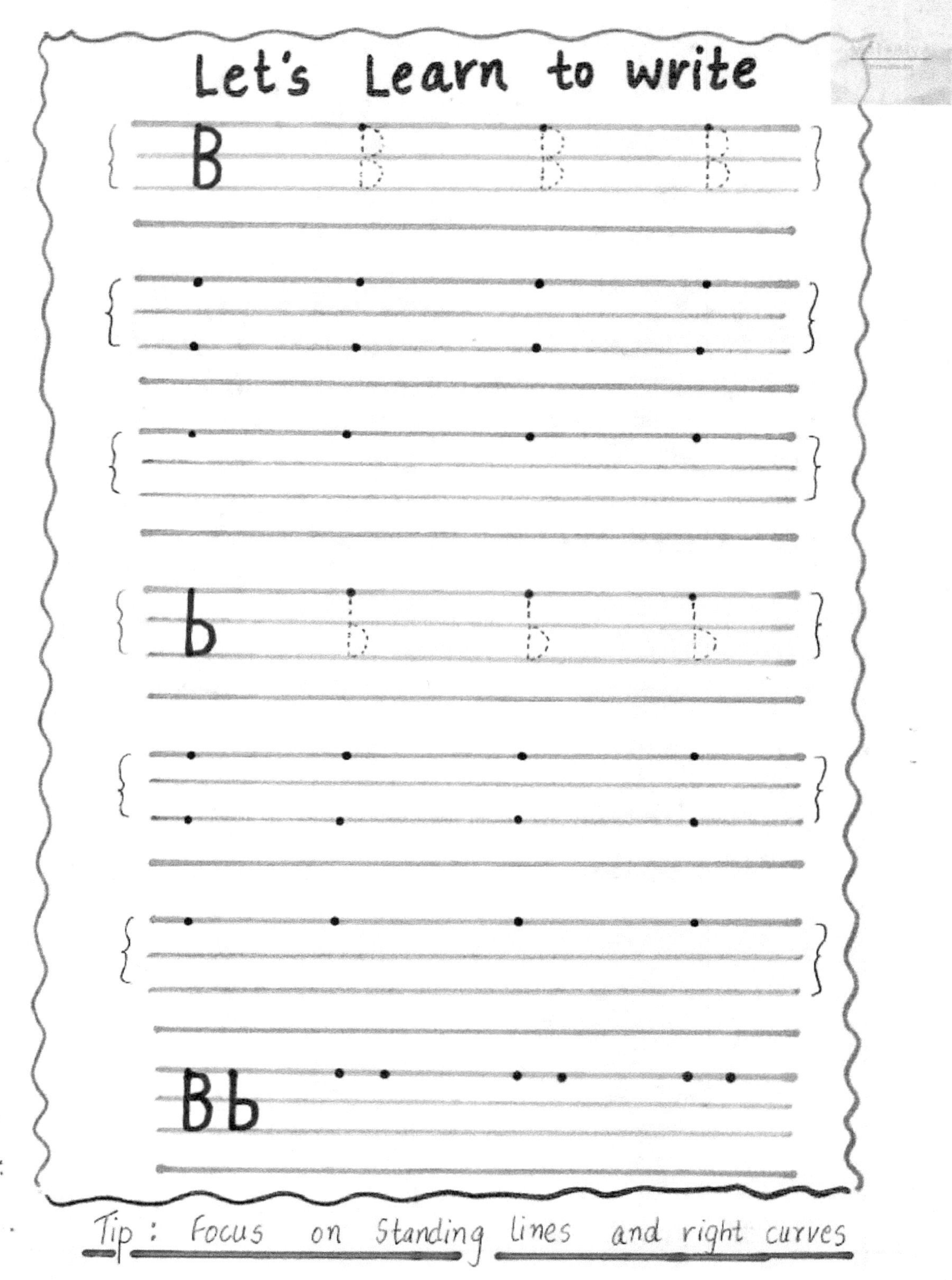

Tip : Focus on standing lines and right curves

LETTER Cc

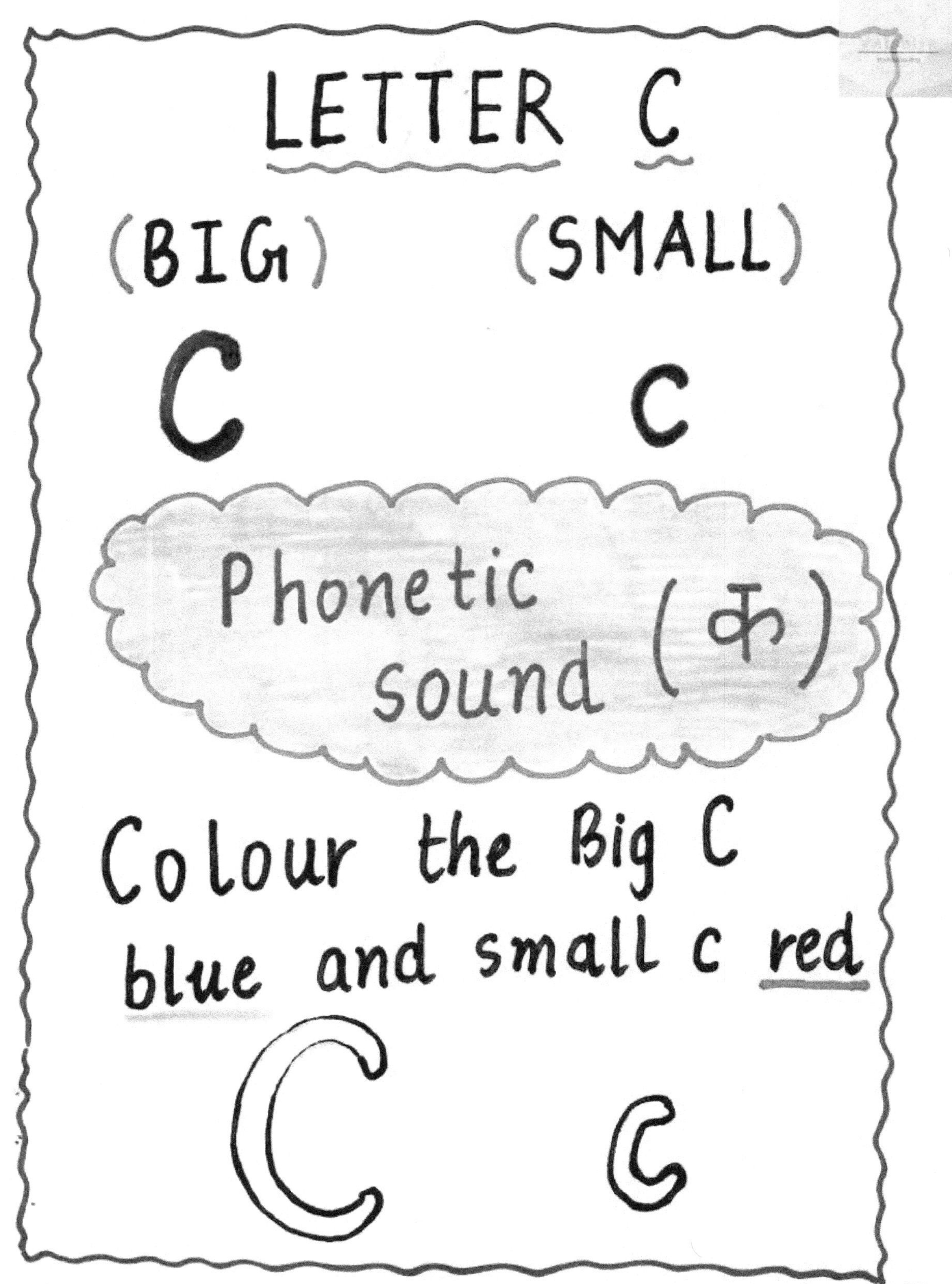

LETTER C
(BIG)
(SMALL)
C
C
Phonetic sound (क)
Colour the Big C blue and small c red
C
C

Things with letter
'C'
Cherry
(क) Cake
(क) Car
(क) Carrot
(क) Caterpillar
(क) Crab

12

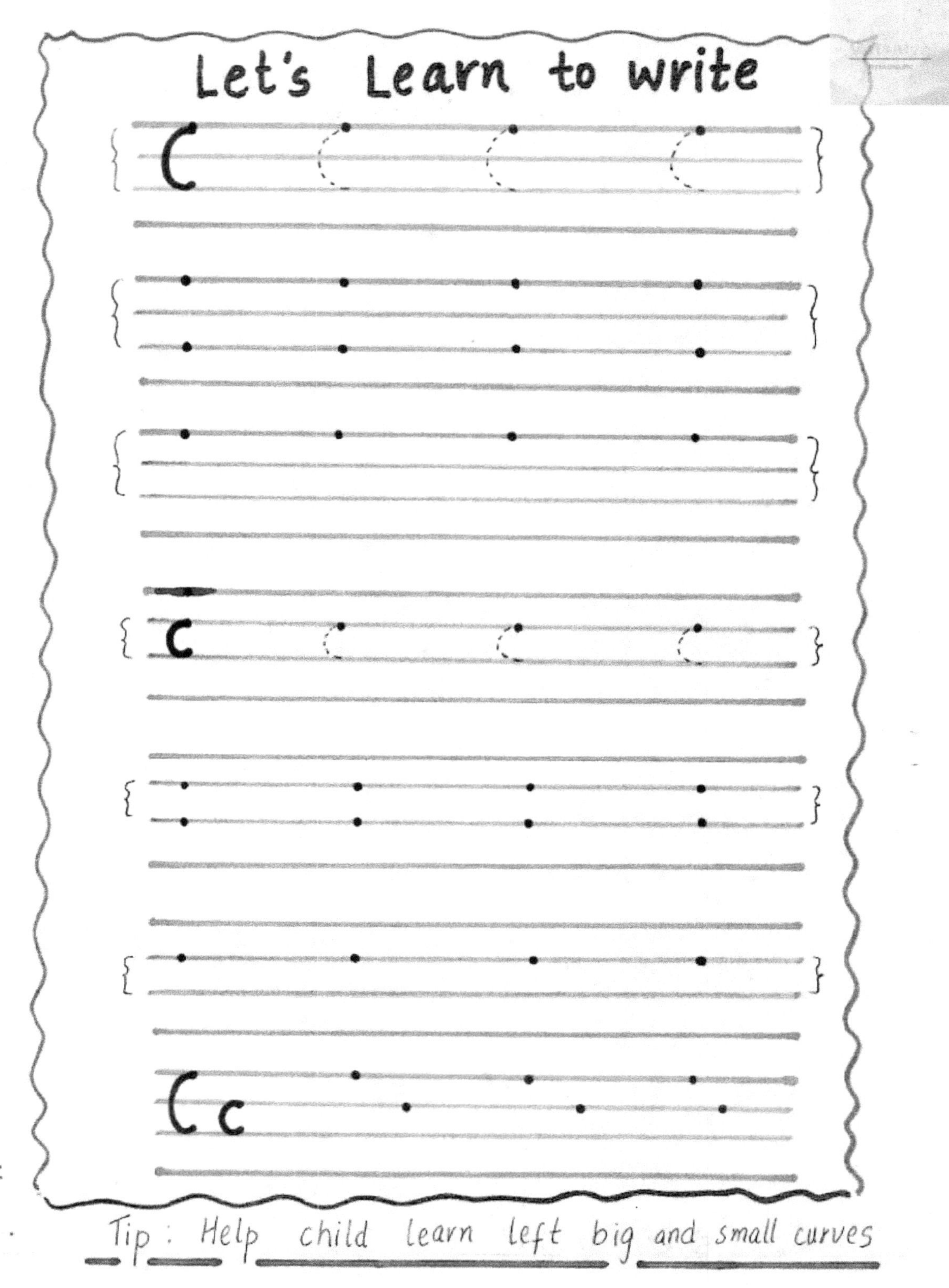

Let's Learn to write
Tip : Help child learn left big and small curves
13

LETTER Dd

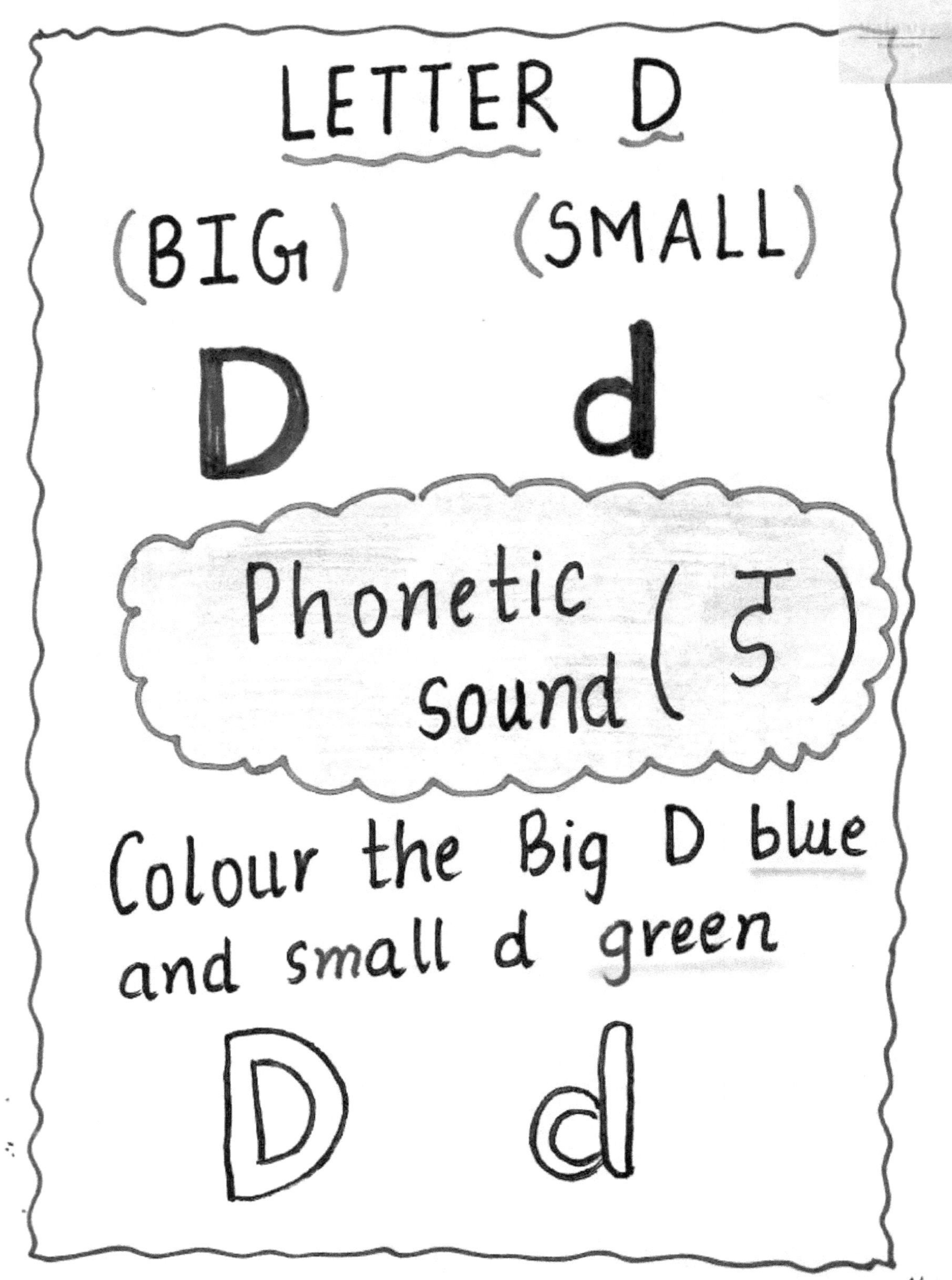
LETTER D
(BIG)
(SMALL)
D
d
Phonetic
sound (ड)
Colour the Big D blue
and small d green
D
d

14

Things with letter 'D'

15

Tip: Explain difference between small b and d

16

LETTER Ee

LETTER E
(BIG)
(SMALL)
E
e
Phonetic sound (ए)
Colour the Big E orange
and small e red
E
e
17

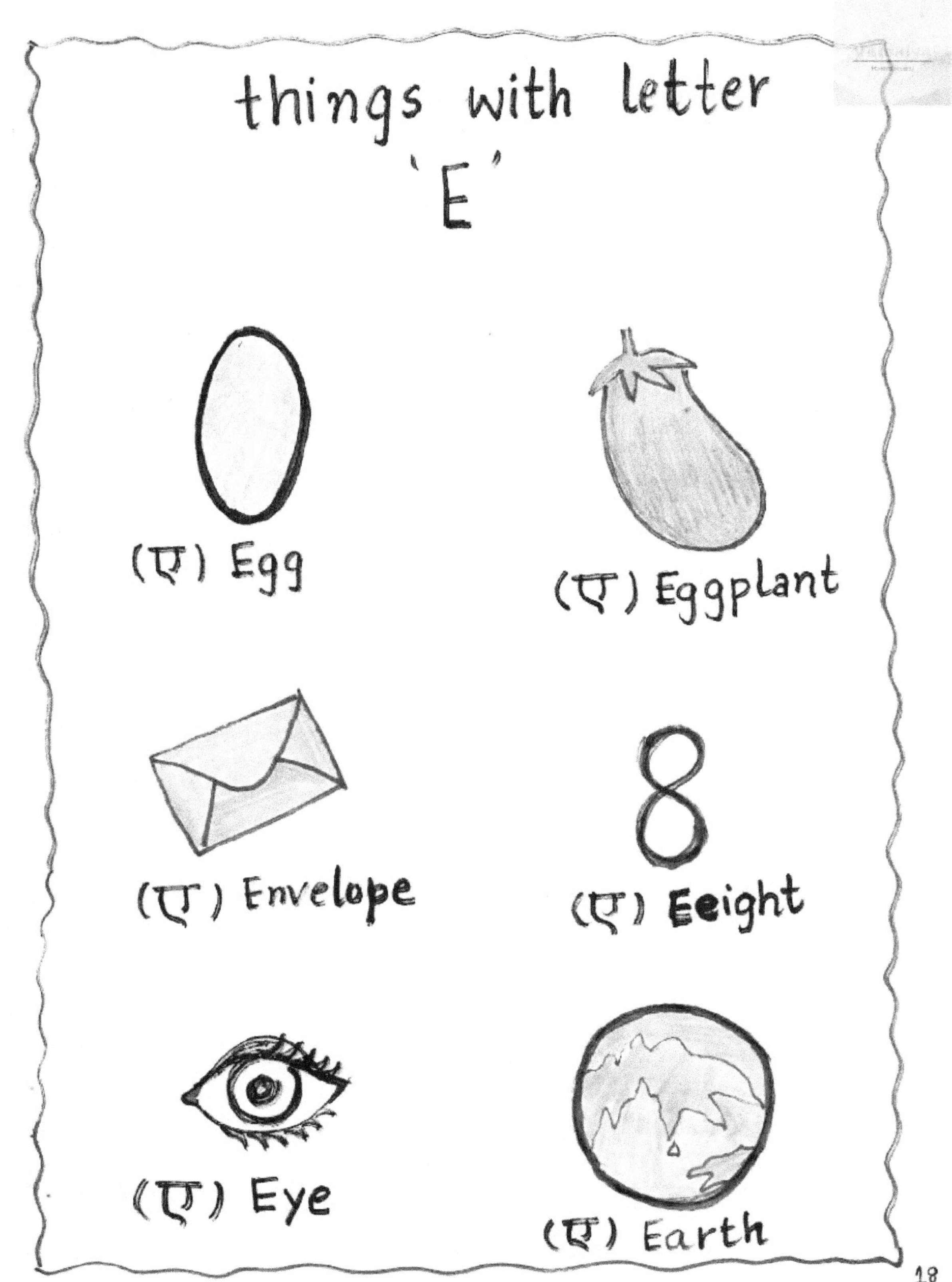

things with letter
'E'
(ए) Egg
(ए) Eggplant
(ए) Envelope
(ए) Eeight
(ए) Eye
(ए) Earth
18

Let's Learn to write

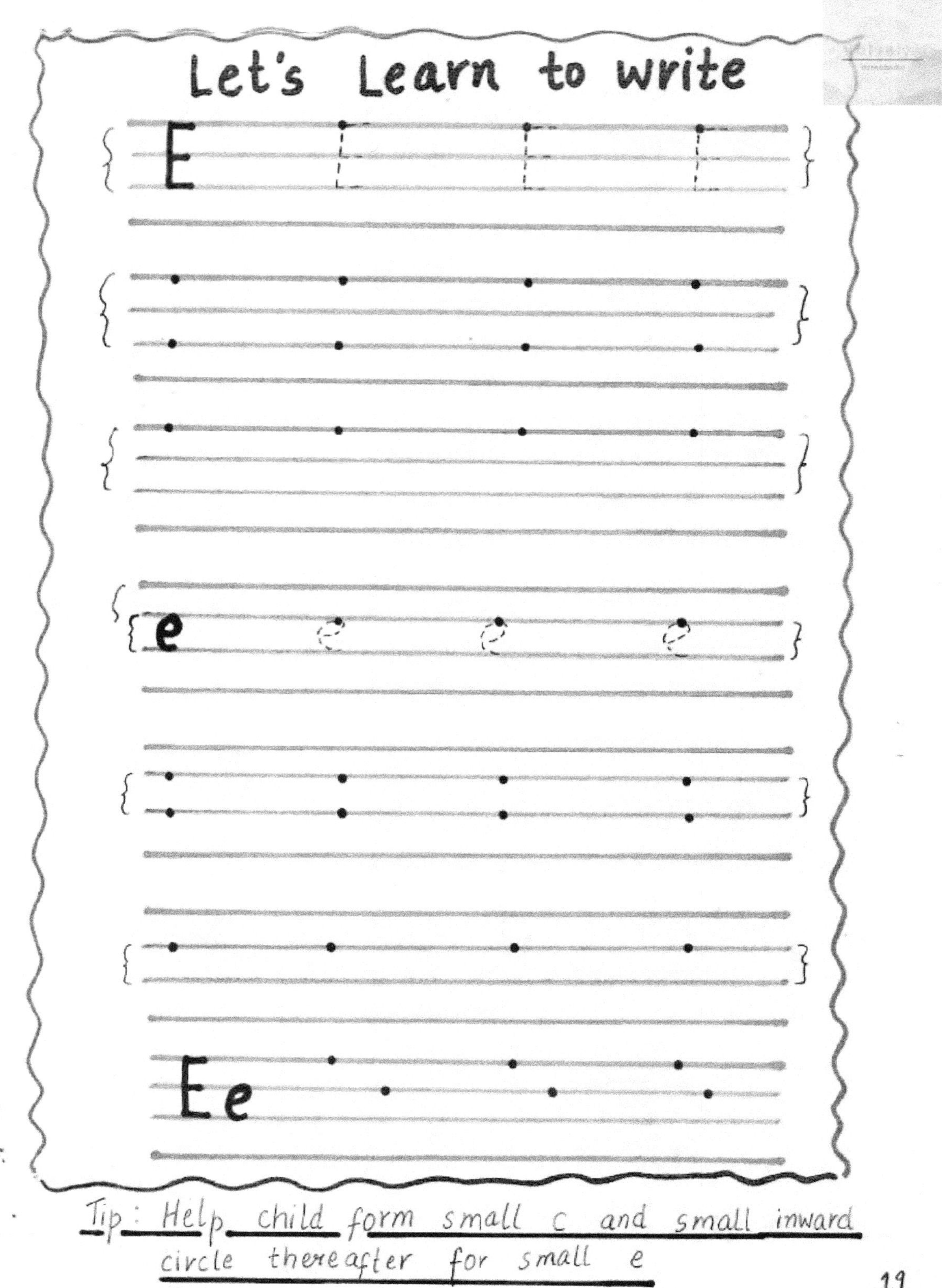

Tip: Help child form small c and small inward circle thereafter for small e

19

LETTER Ff

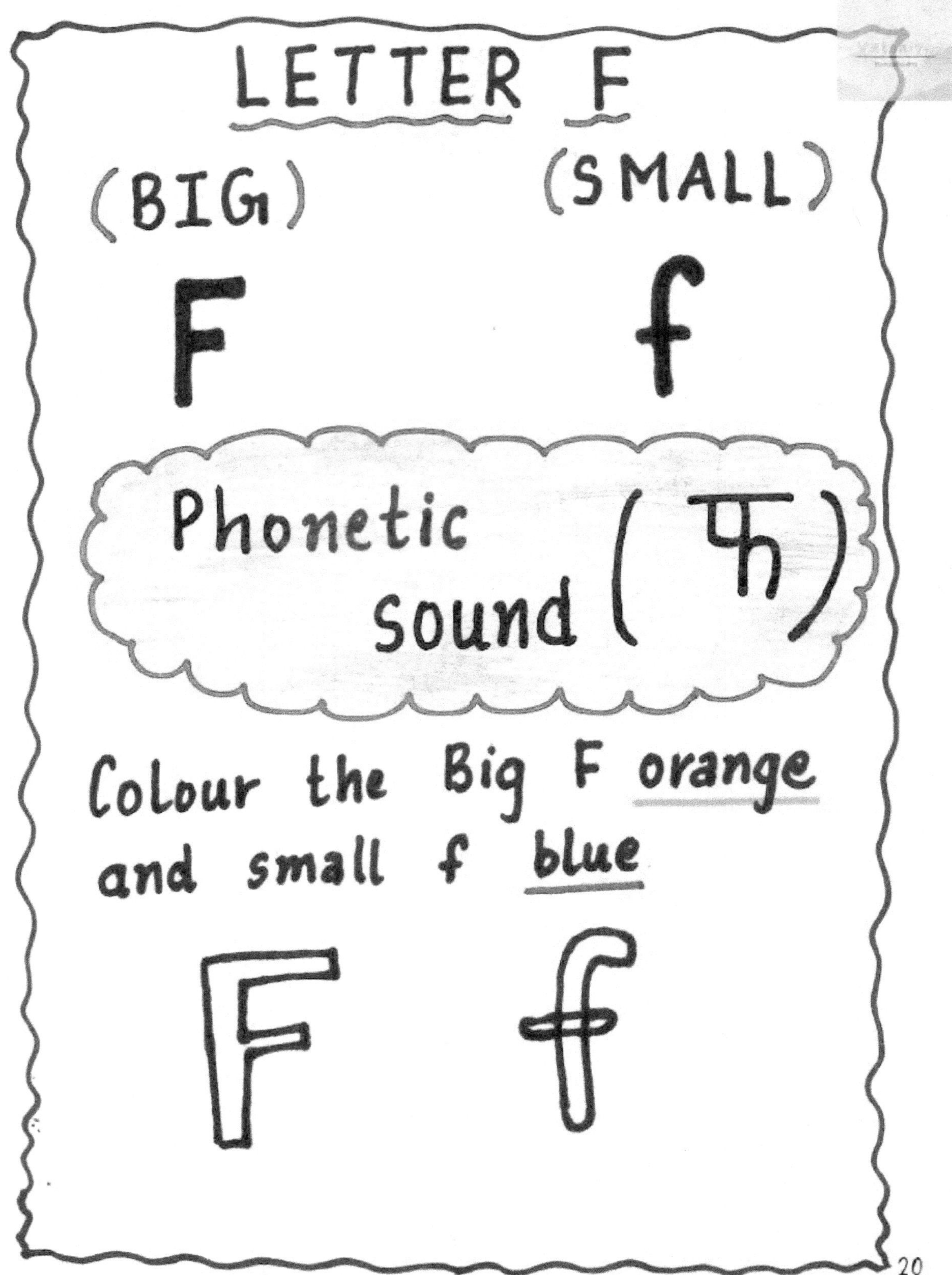

LETTER F
(BIG)
(SMALL)
F
f
Phonetic sound (फ)
Colour the Big F orange and small f blue
20

21

Tip: Start with the curve on red line for f

22

LETTER Gg

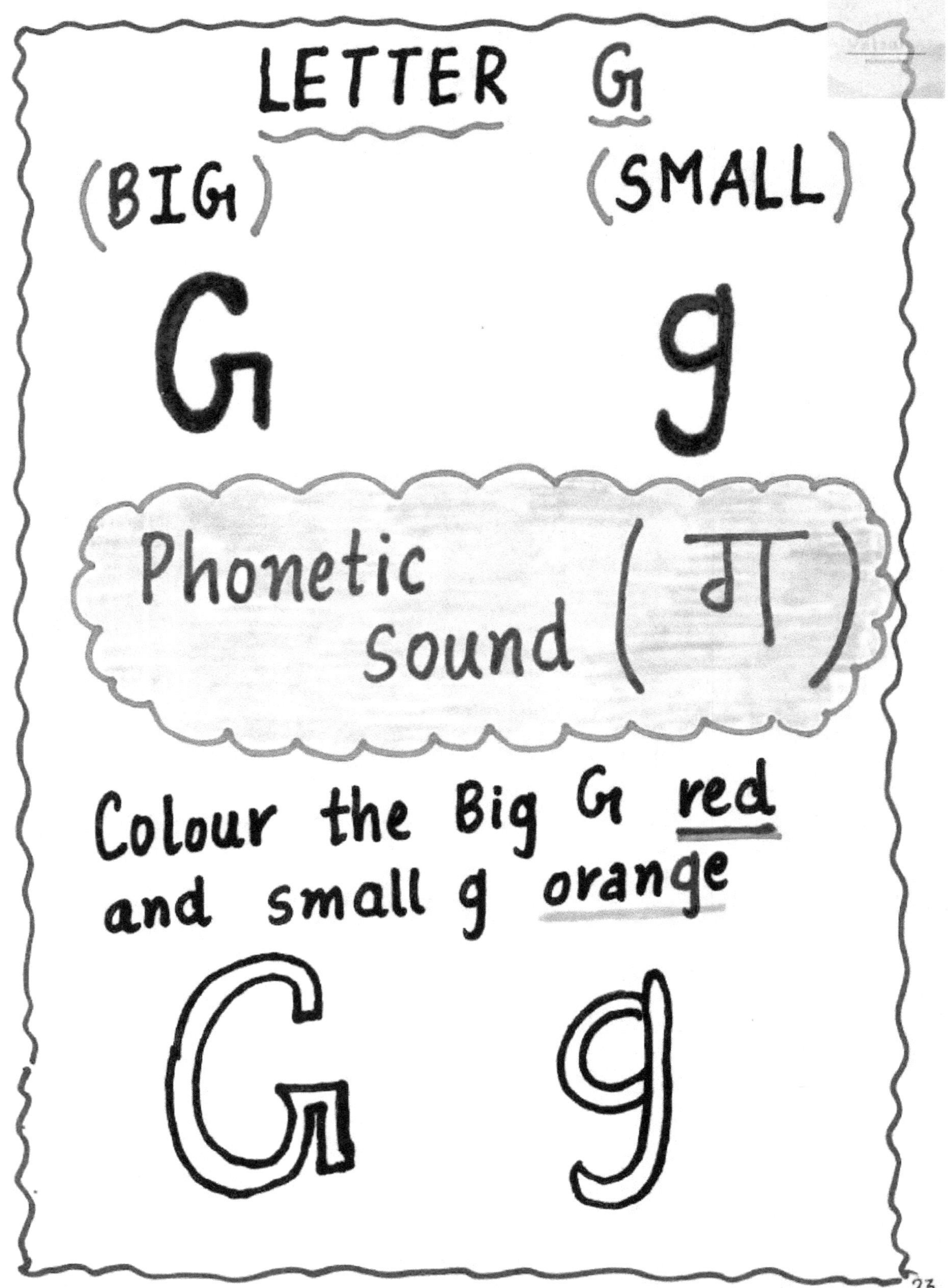

LETTER G
(BIG)
(SMALL)
G
g
Phonetic Sound (ग)
Colour the Big G red and small g orange

things with letter 'G'

(π) Gloves

(π) Grapes

(π) Gate

(π) Ghost

(π) Glass

(π) Grass

24

Tip: Introduce the child to bottom three lines for small g

25

LETTER Hh

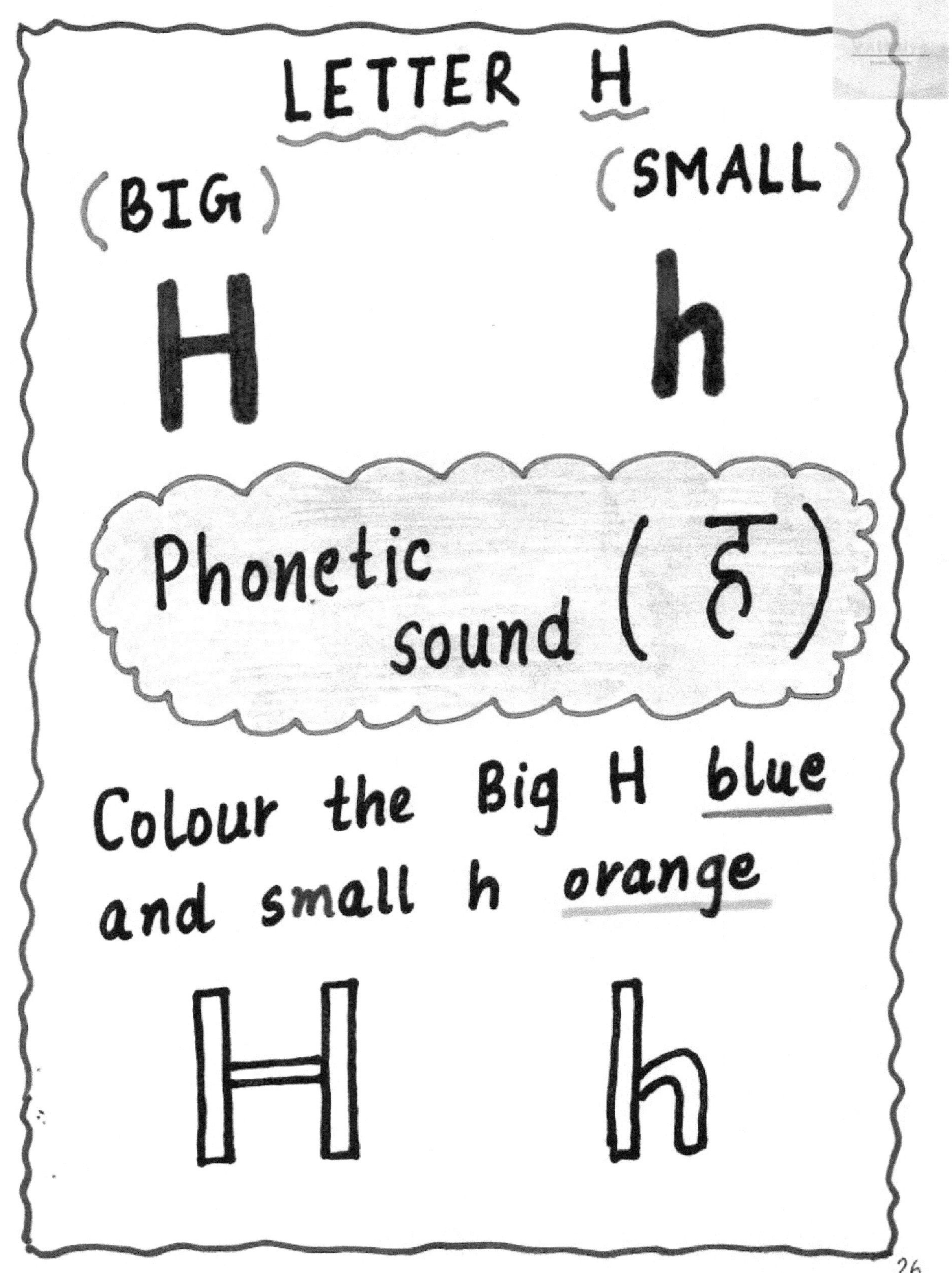

LETTER H
(BIG)
(SMALL)
H
h
Phonetic sound (ह)
Colour the Big H blue and small h orange
H h
26

things with letter
'H'
(ह) Hat
(ह) House
(ह) Heart
(ह) Helicopter
(ह) Hammer
(ह) Hen
27

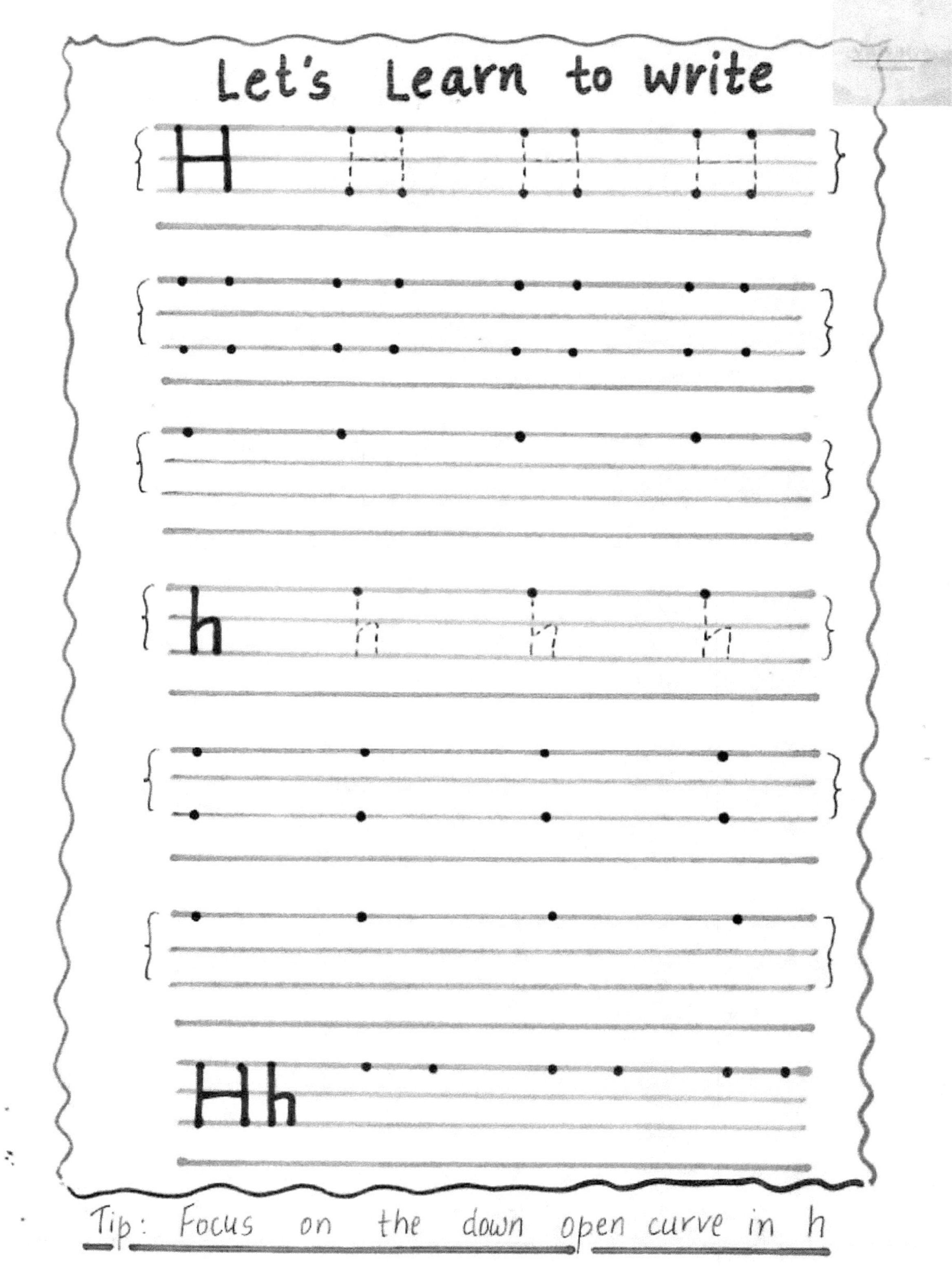

Tip: Focus on the down open curve in h

28

LETTER Ii

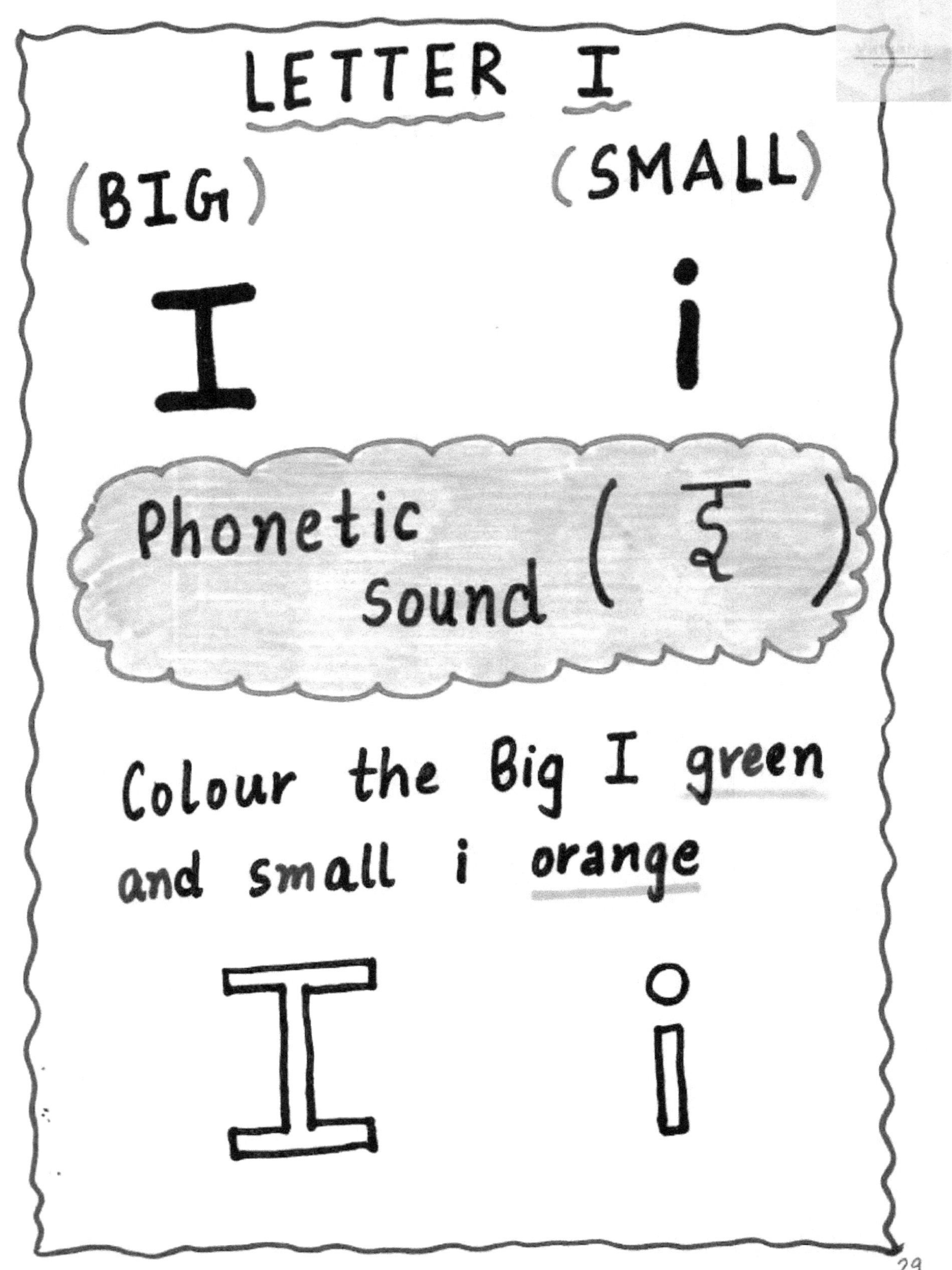

LETTER I
(BIG)
(SMALL)
I
i
Phonetic Sound (ई)
Colour the Big I green and small i orange

29

things with letter
'I'
(इ) Ice cream
(इ) Igloo
(इ) Ice
(इ) Island
(इ) Ink
(इ) Insect

Let's Learn to write

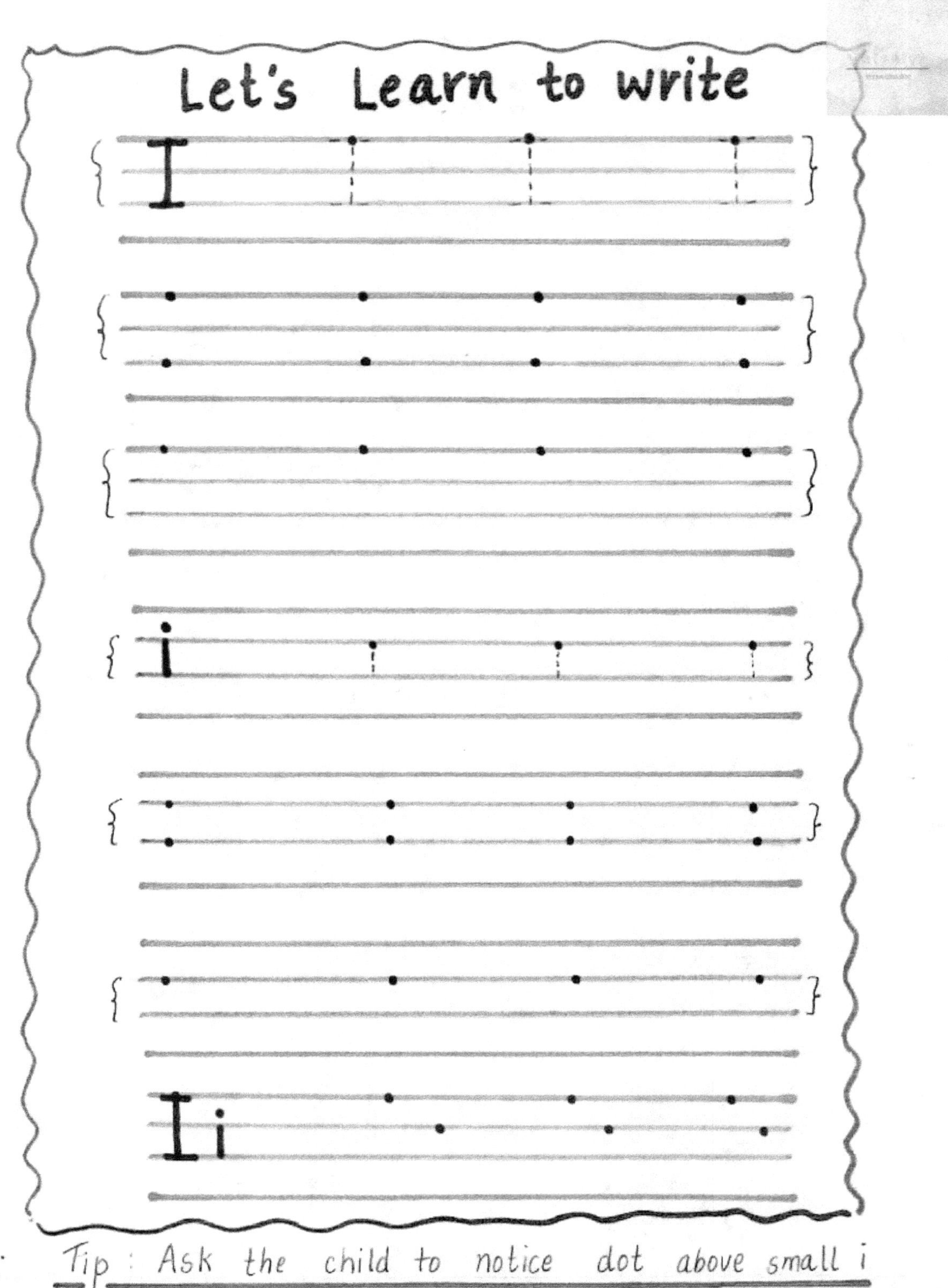

Tip : Ask the child to notice dot above small i

LETTER Jj

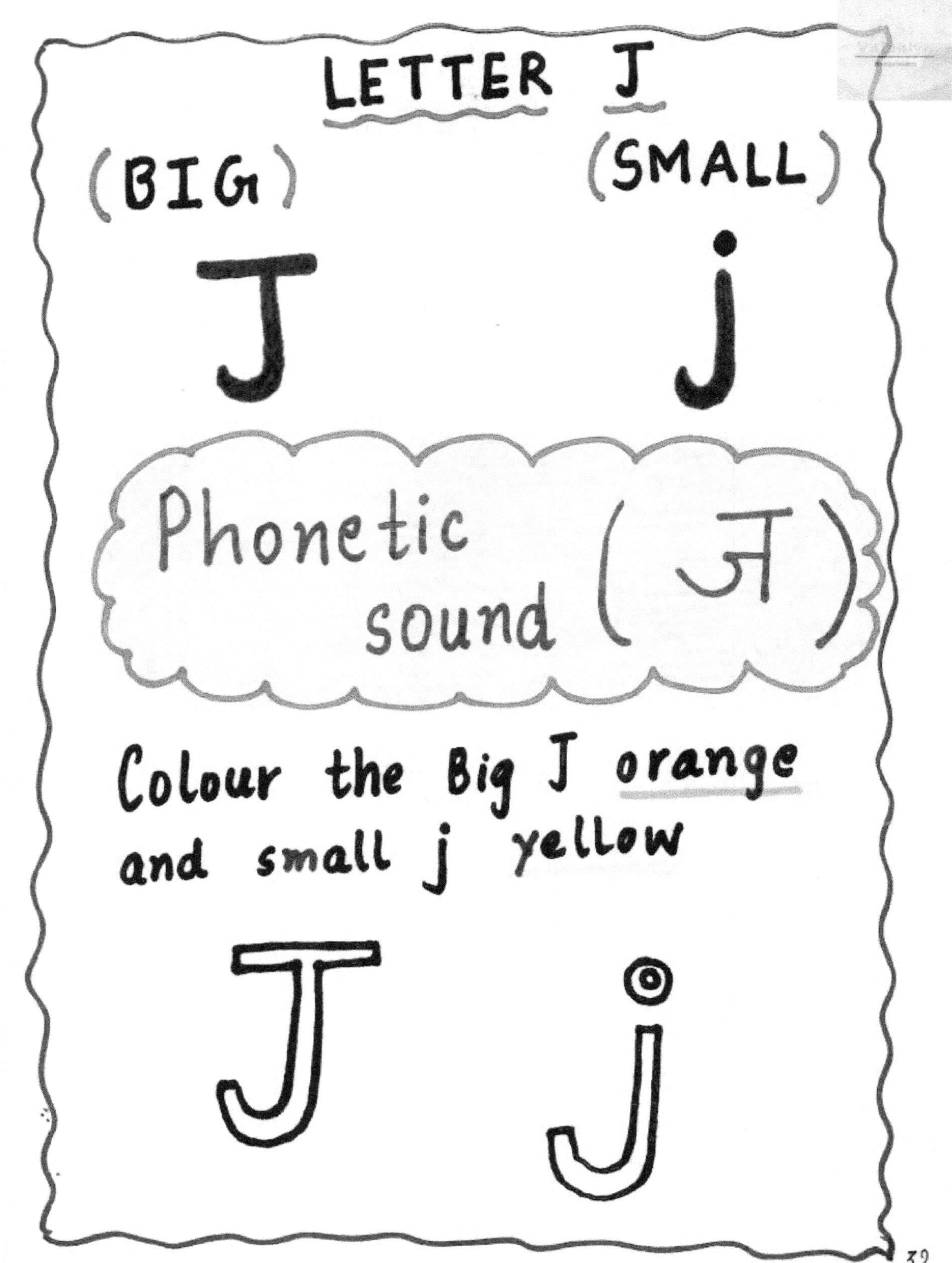
LETTER J
(BIG)
(SMALL)
J
j
Phonetic sound (ज)
Colour the Big J orange
and small j yellow
J
j
32

things with letter 'J'

33

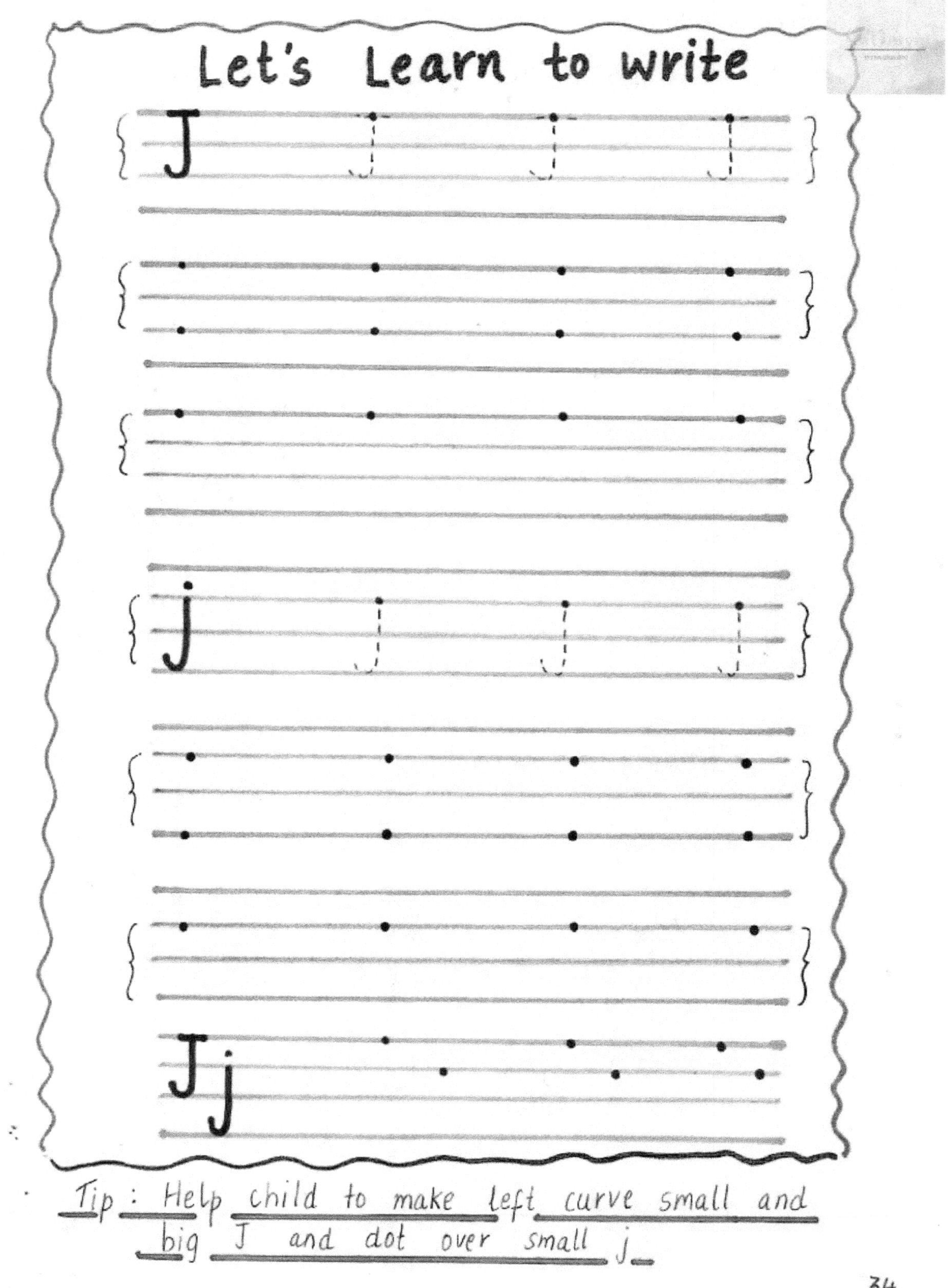

Tip : Help child to make left curve small and big J and dot over small j

34

LETTER Kk

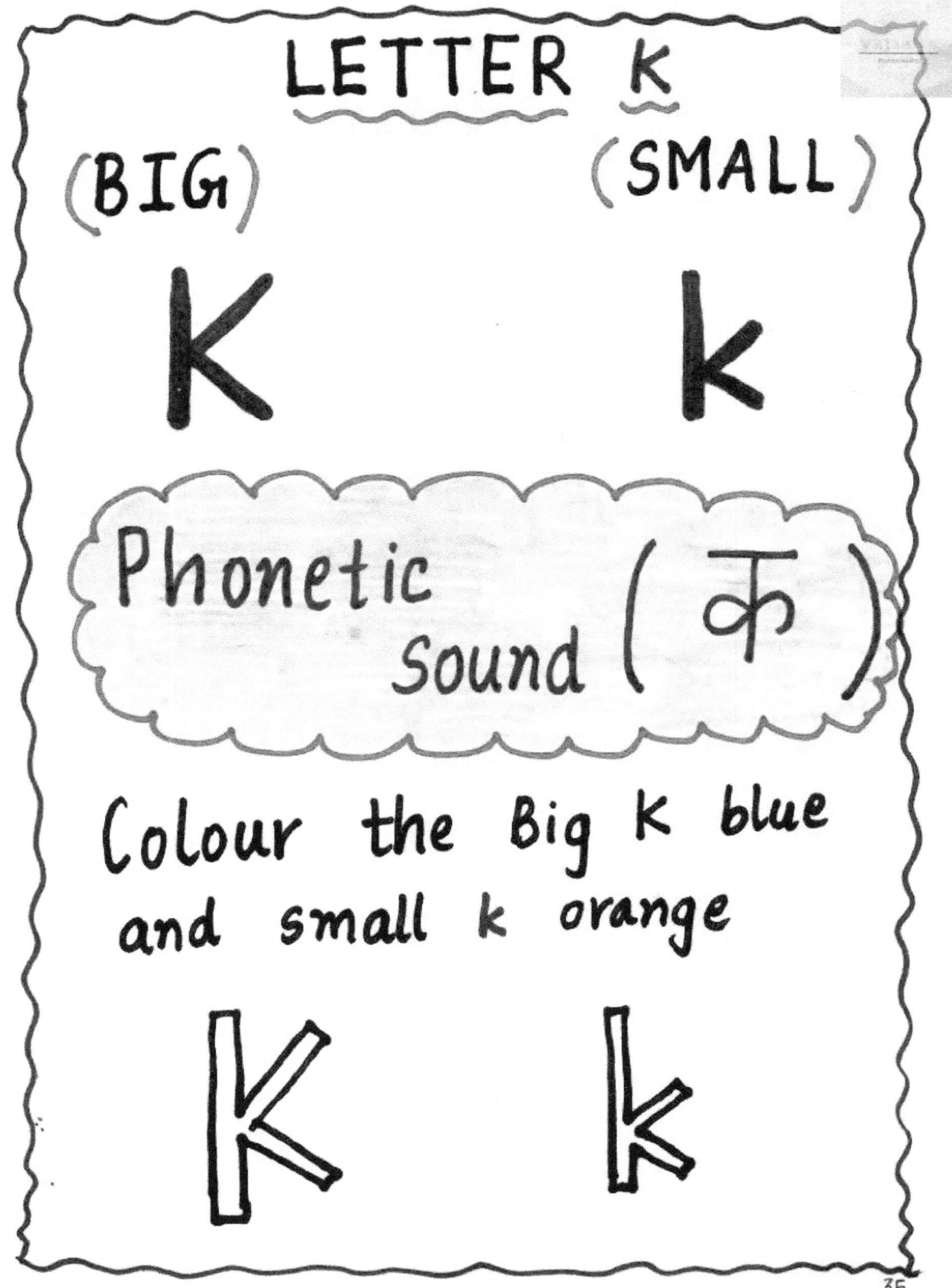

LETTER k
(BIG)
(SMALL)
K
k
Phonetic Sound (क)
Colour the Big K blue and small k orange
K
k
35

things with letter 'K'

36

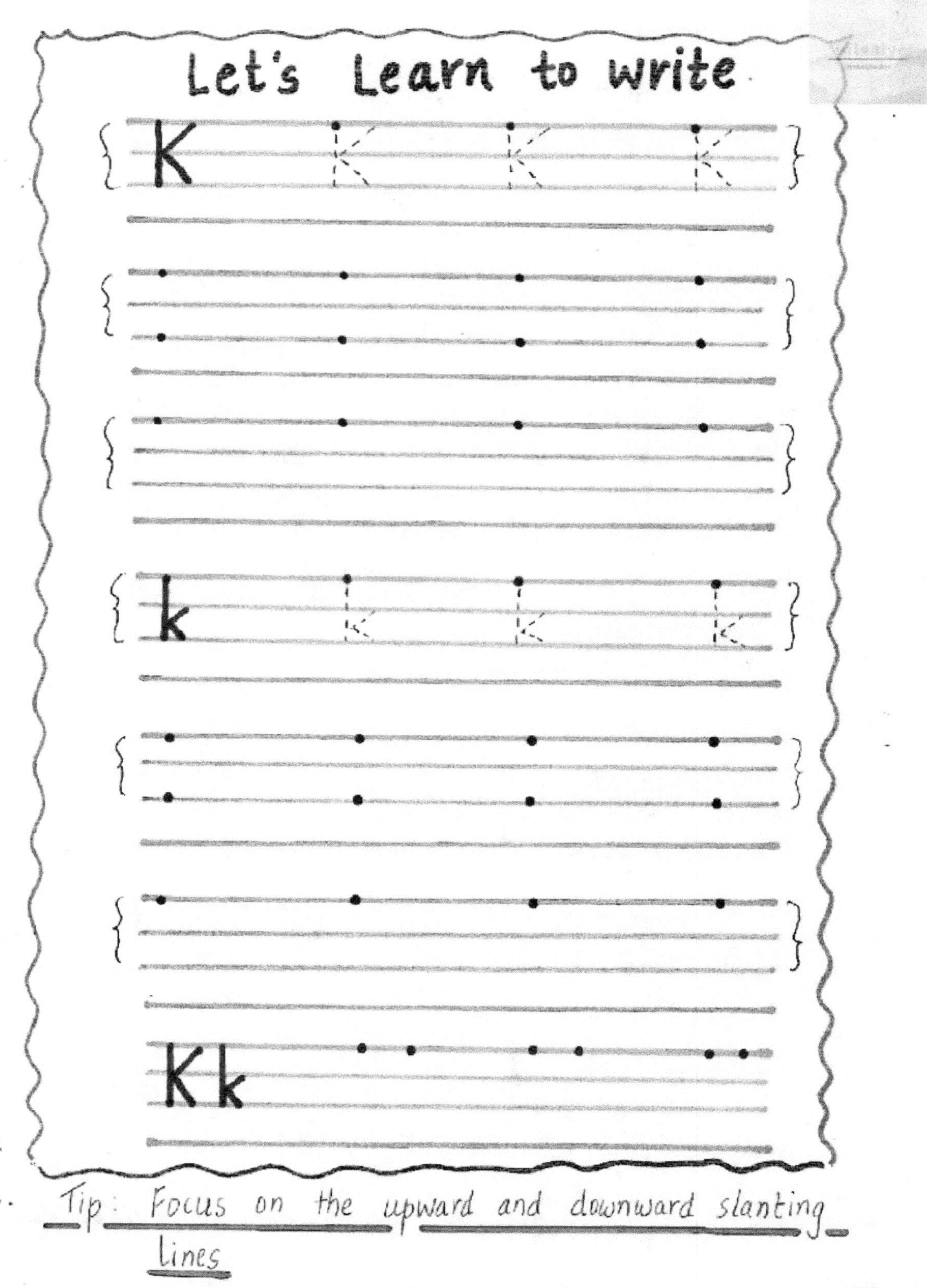

Tip: Focus on the upward and downward slanting lines

LETTER LI

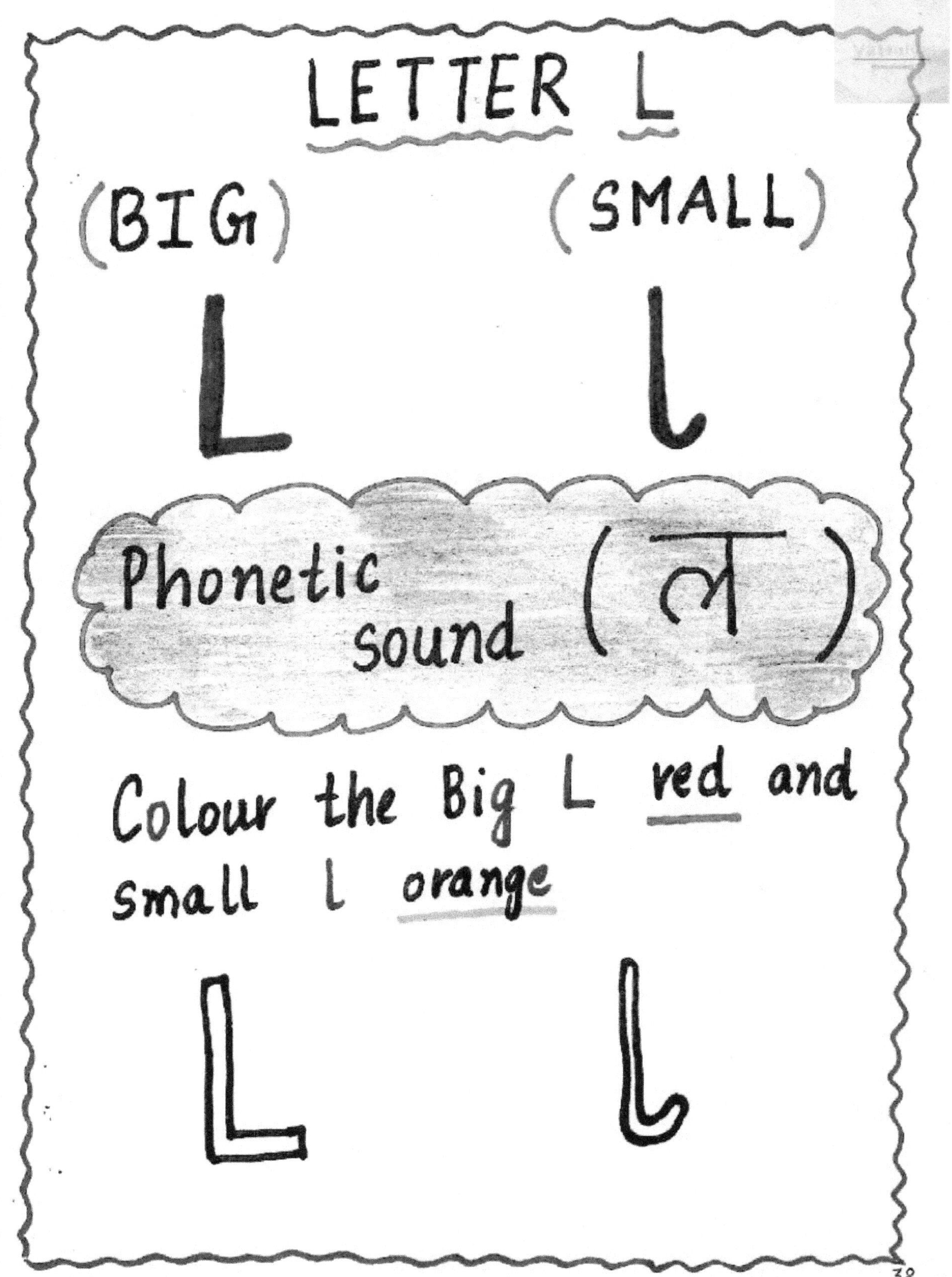

LETTER L
(BIG)
(SMALL)
L
l
Phonetic sound (ल)
Colour the Big L red and small l orange

things with letter 'L'
(ल) Leaf
(ल) Lamp
(ल) Lemon
(ल) Lava
(ल) Lips
(ल) Lollipop

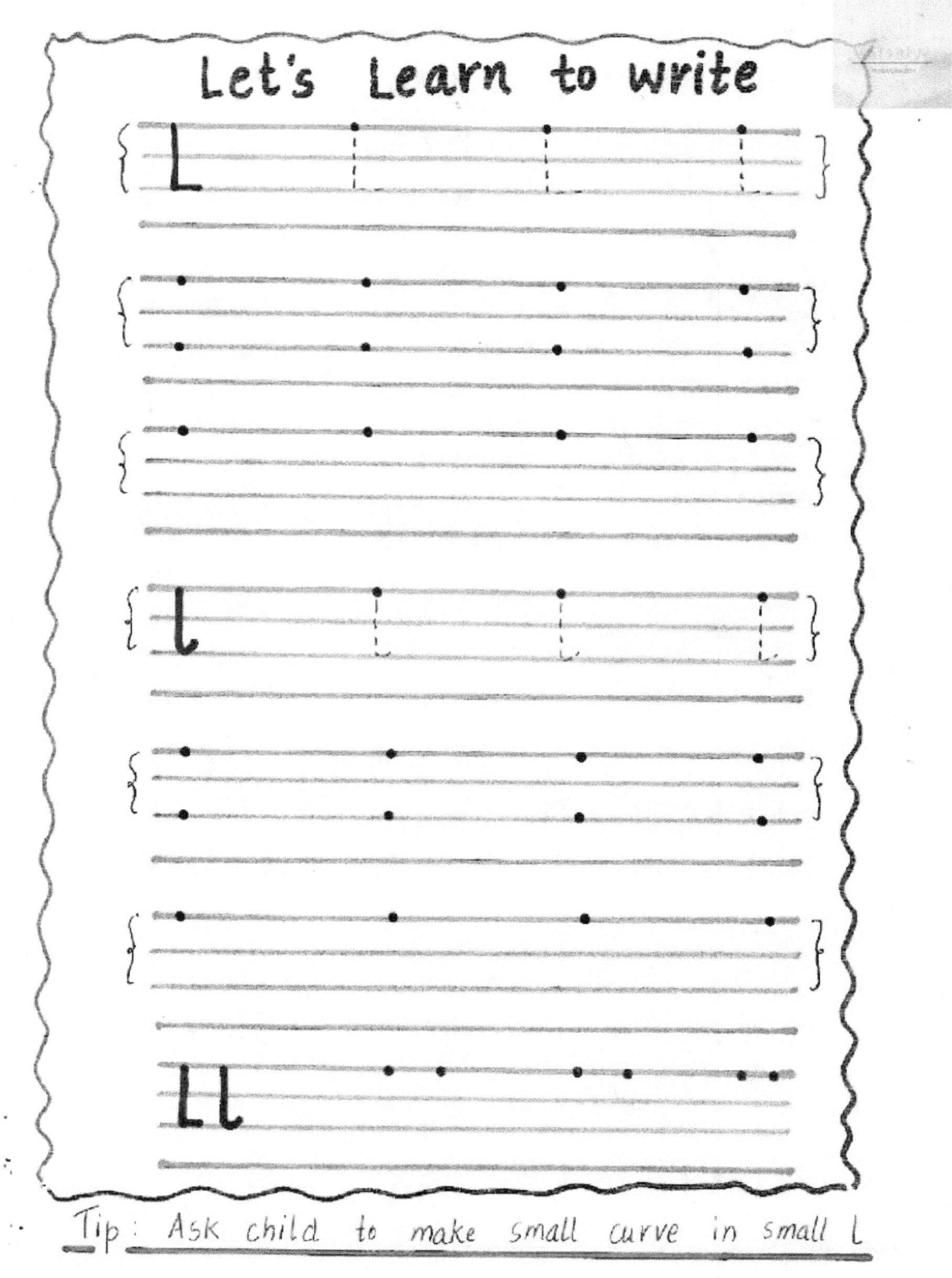

Tip: Ask child to make small curve in small l

40

LETTER Mm

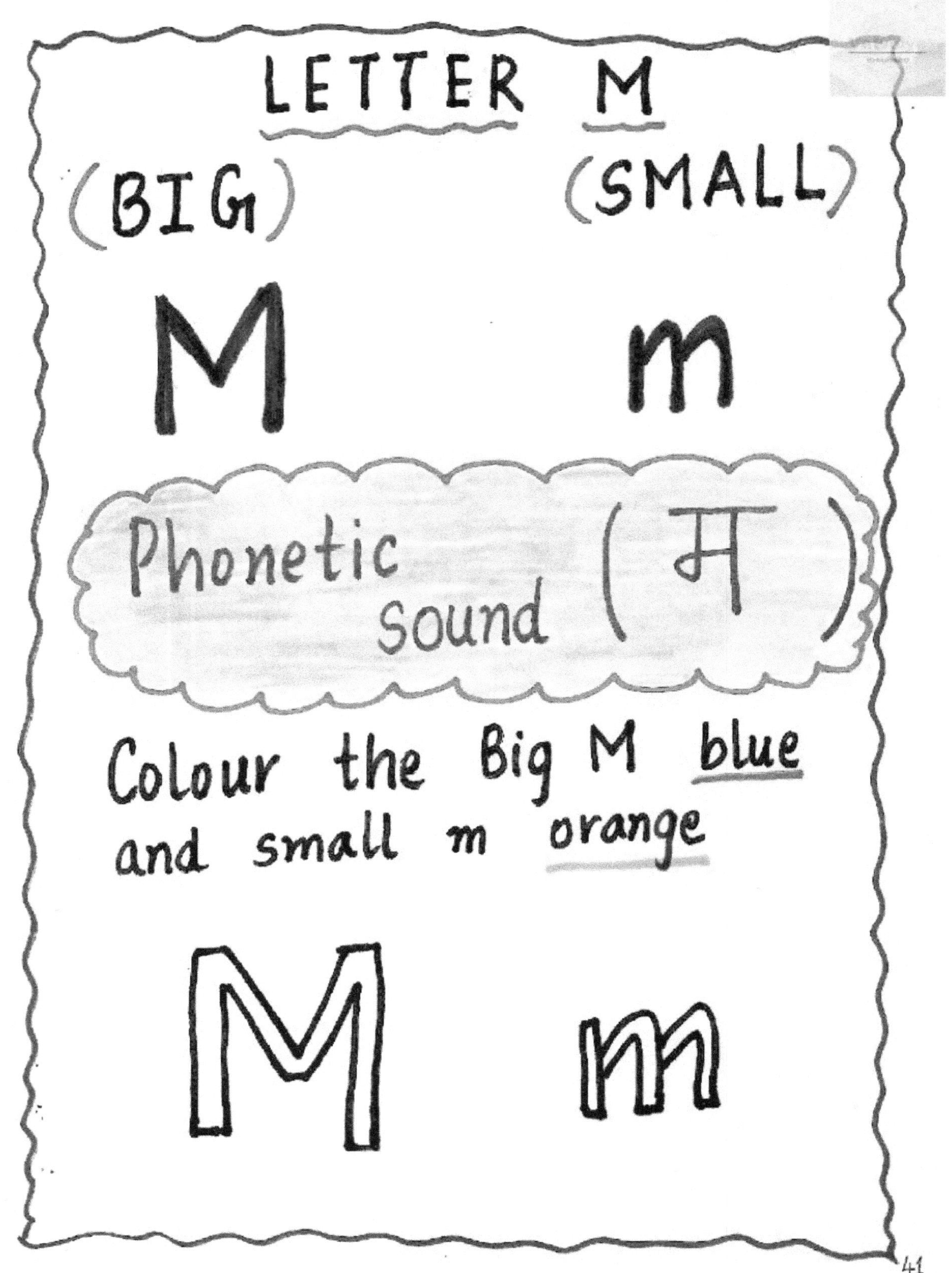

LETTER M
(BIG)
(SMALL)
M
m
Phonetic Sound (म)
Colour the Big M blue
and small m orange
M
m
41

things with letter 'M'

(म) Moon

(म) Mug

(म) Mushroom

(म) Monkey

(म) Mango

(म) Mop

42

Let's Learn to write

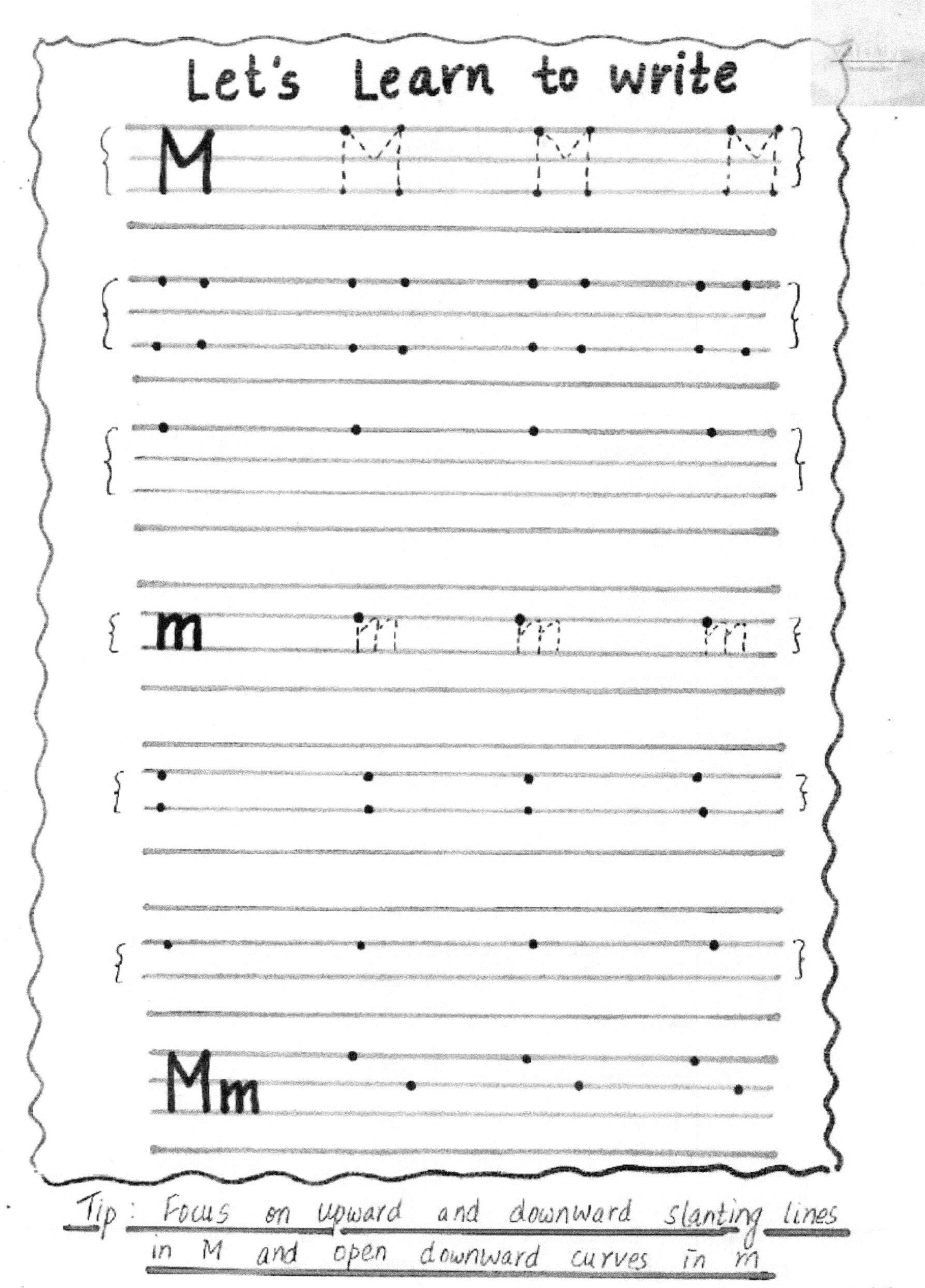

Tip: Focus on upward and downward slanting lines in M and open downward curves in m

43

LETTER Nn

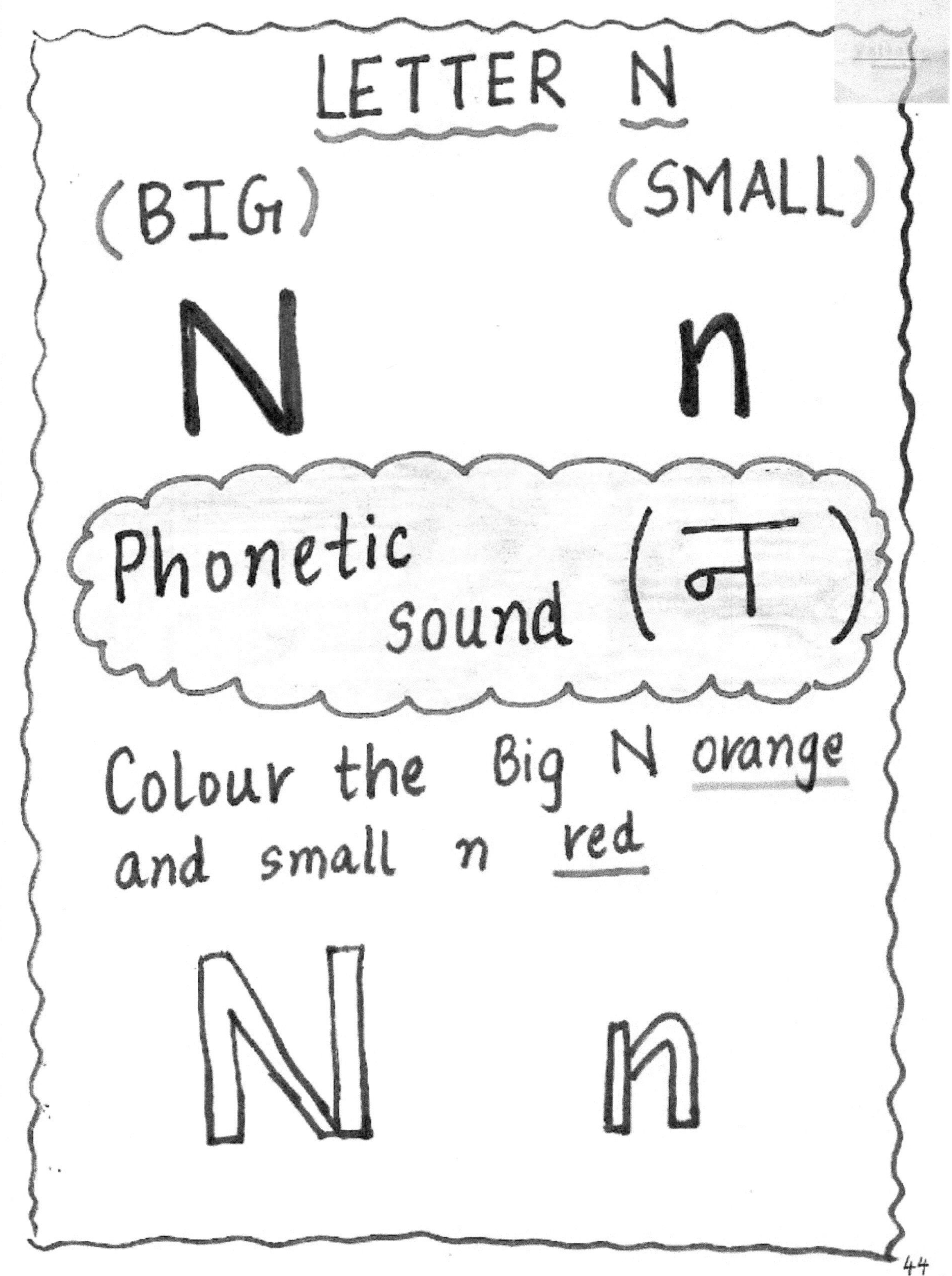

LETTER N

(BIG)   (SMALL)

N   n

Phonetic sound (न)

Colour the Big N orange
and small n red

N   n

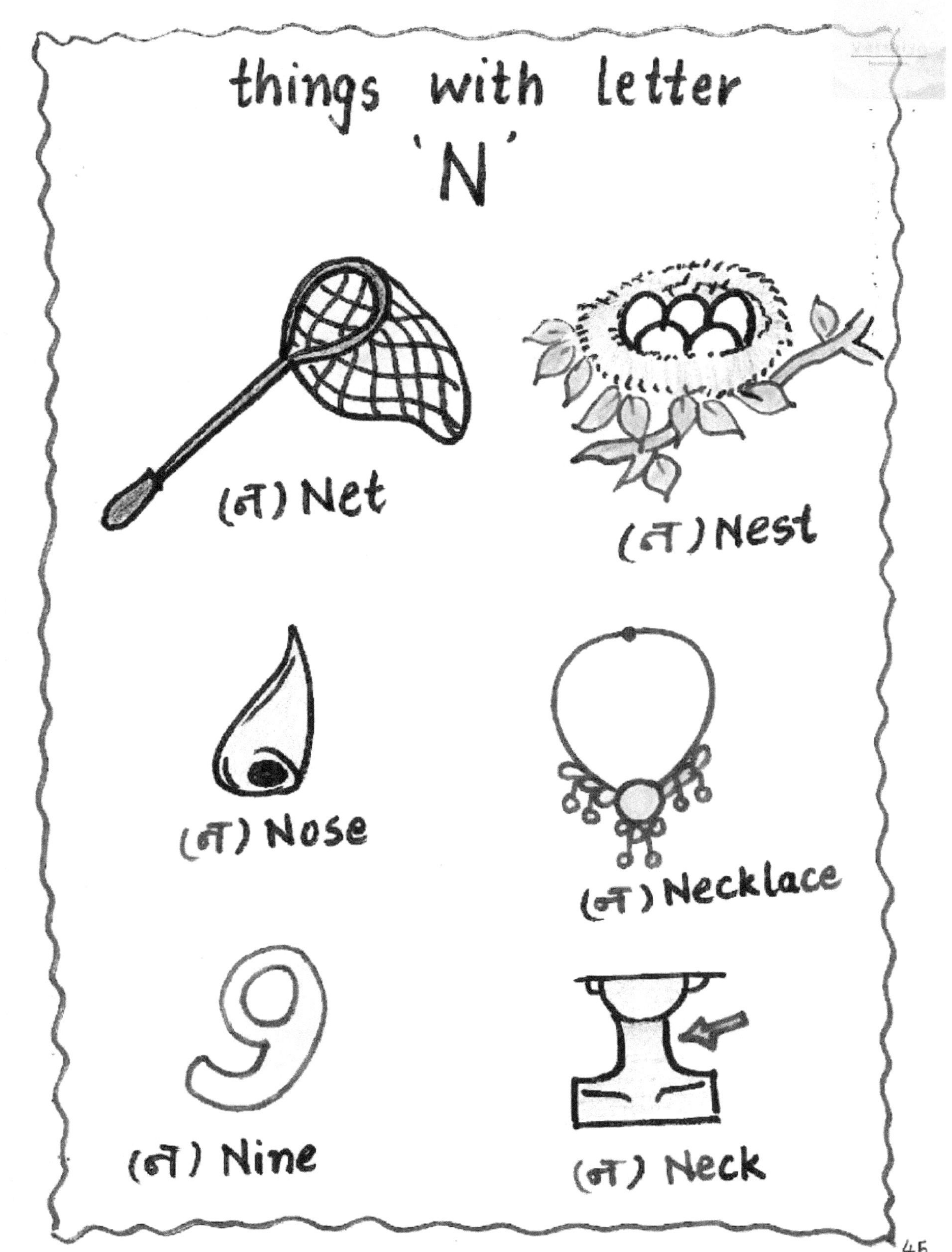

things with letter
'N'
(न) Net
(न) Nest
(न) Nose
(न) Necklace
(न) Nine
(न) Neck
45

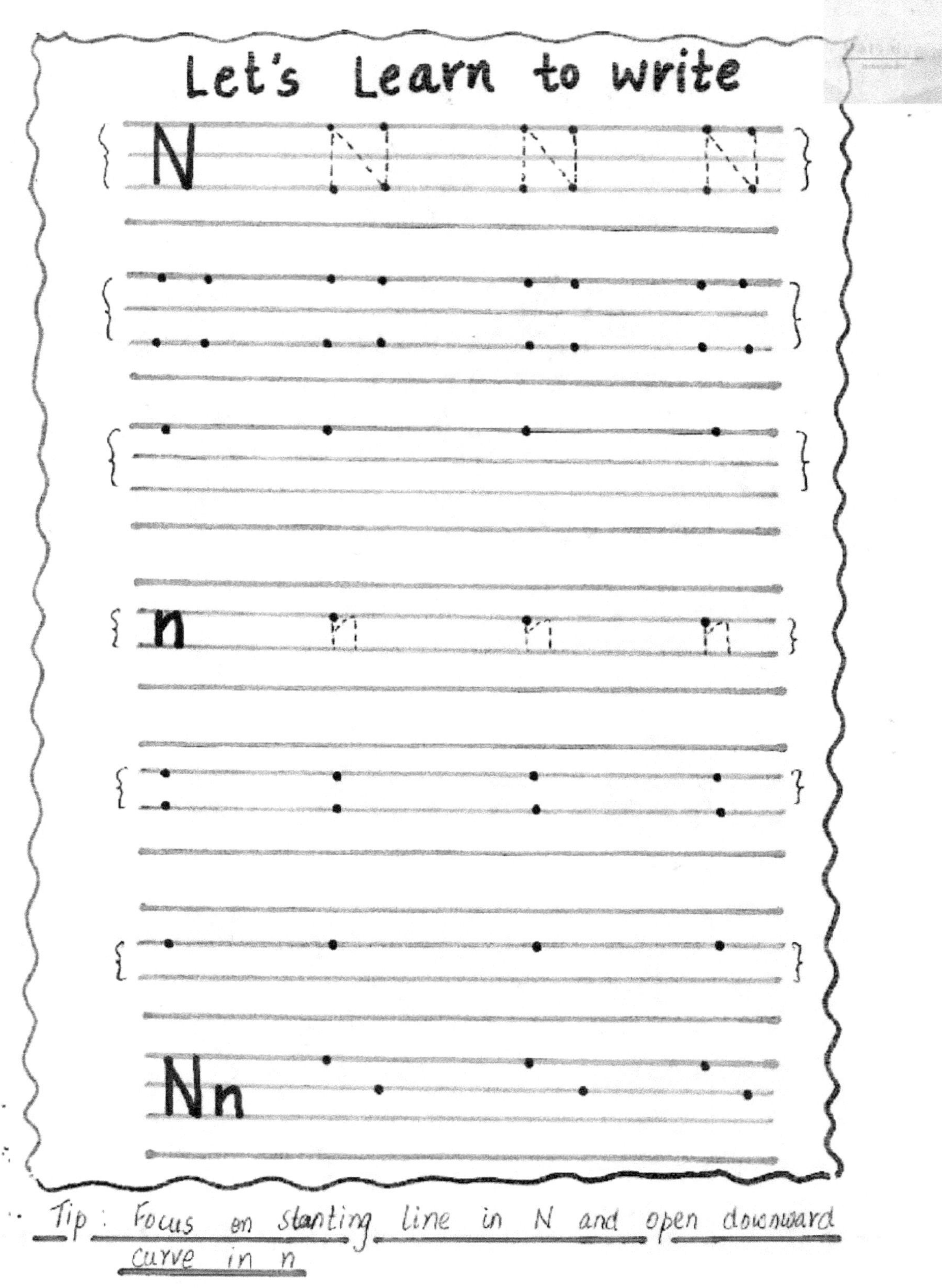

Tip: Focus on slanting line in N and open downward curve in n

LETTER Oo

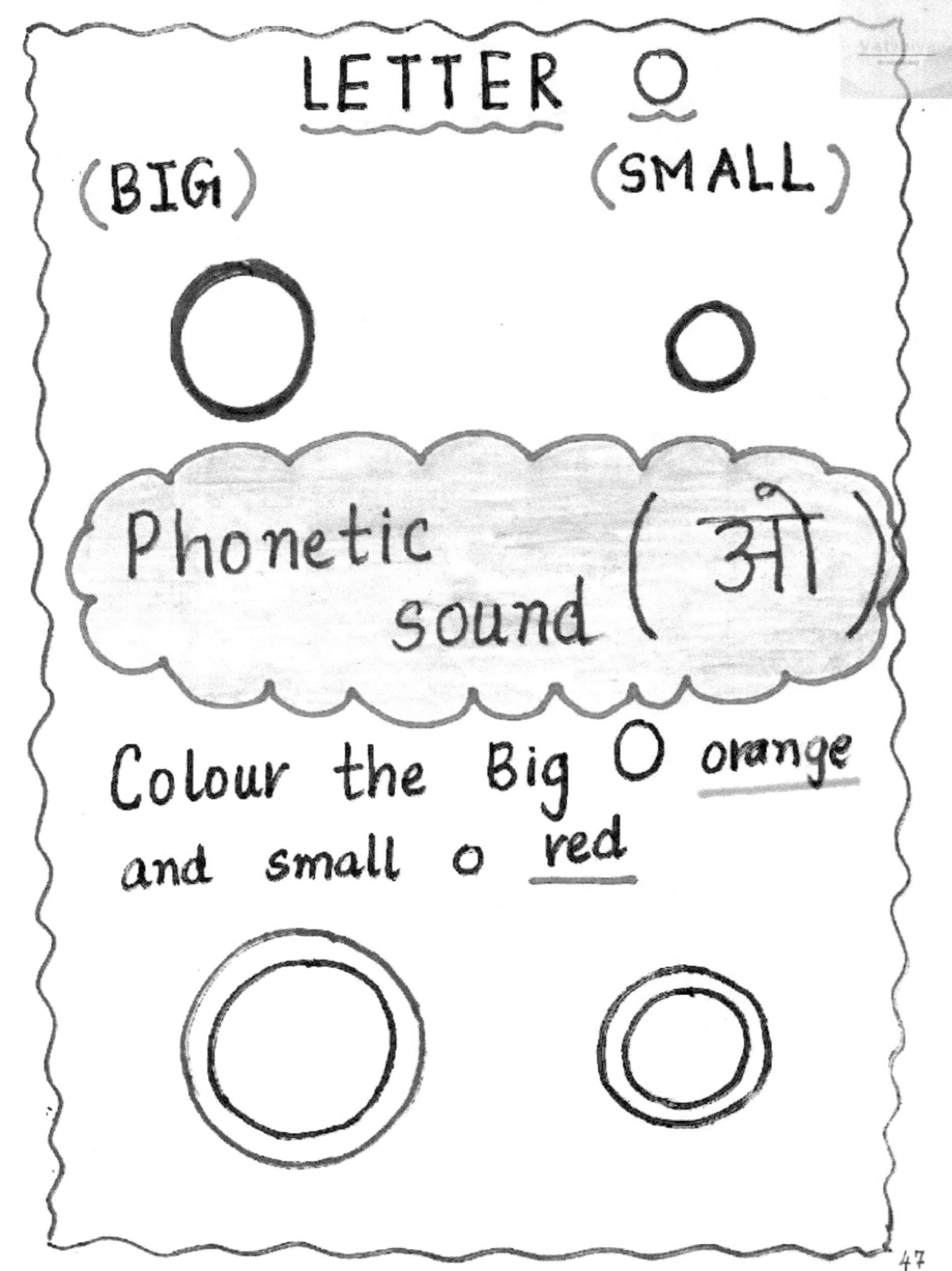

LETTER O
(BIG)
(SMALL)
Phonetic sound (ओ)
Colour the Big O orange
and small o red
47

things with letter
'O'
(ओ) Olive
(ओ) Octopus
(ओ) Orange
(ओ) Owl
(ओ) Ocean
(ओ) Onion
48

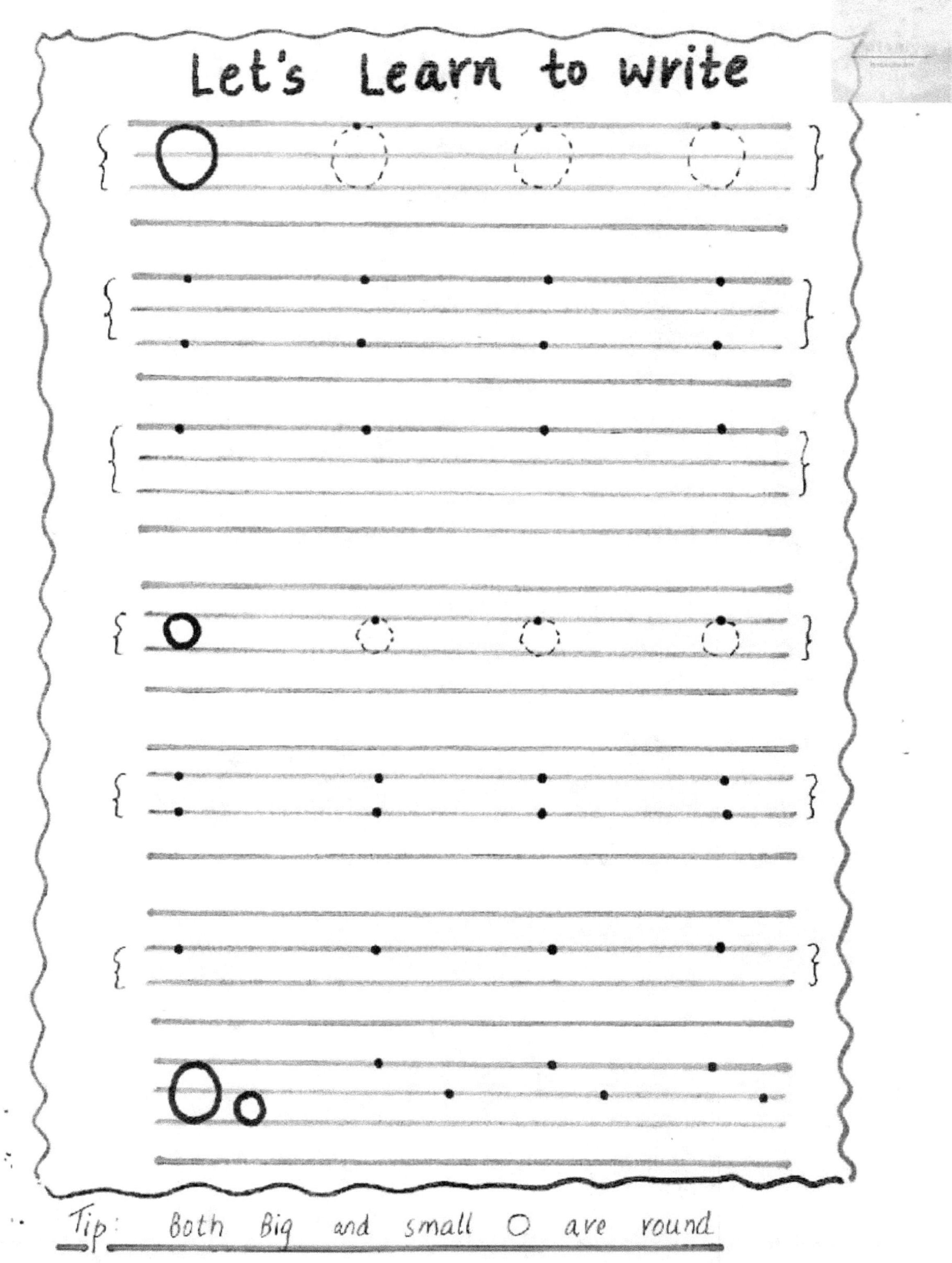

Tip: Both Big and small O are round

49

LETTER Pp

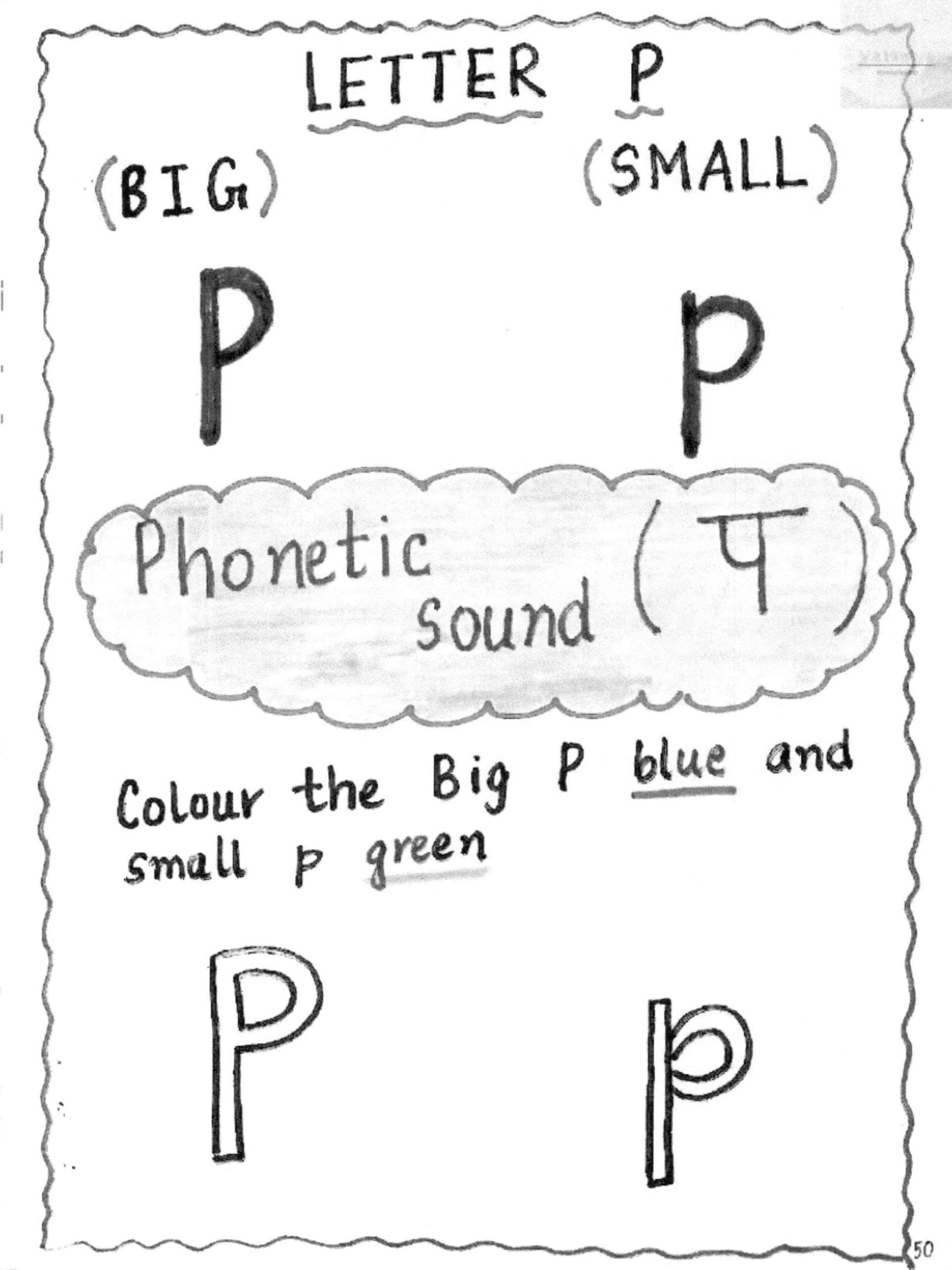
LETTER P
(BIG)
(SMALL)
P
P
Phonetic sound (प)
Colour the Big P blue and small p green
P
p
50

things with letter
'P'
(प) Pear
(प) Panda
(प) Pencil
(प) Pizza
(प) Pan
(प) Plant
51

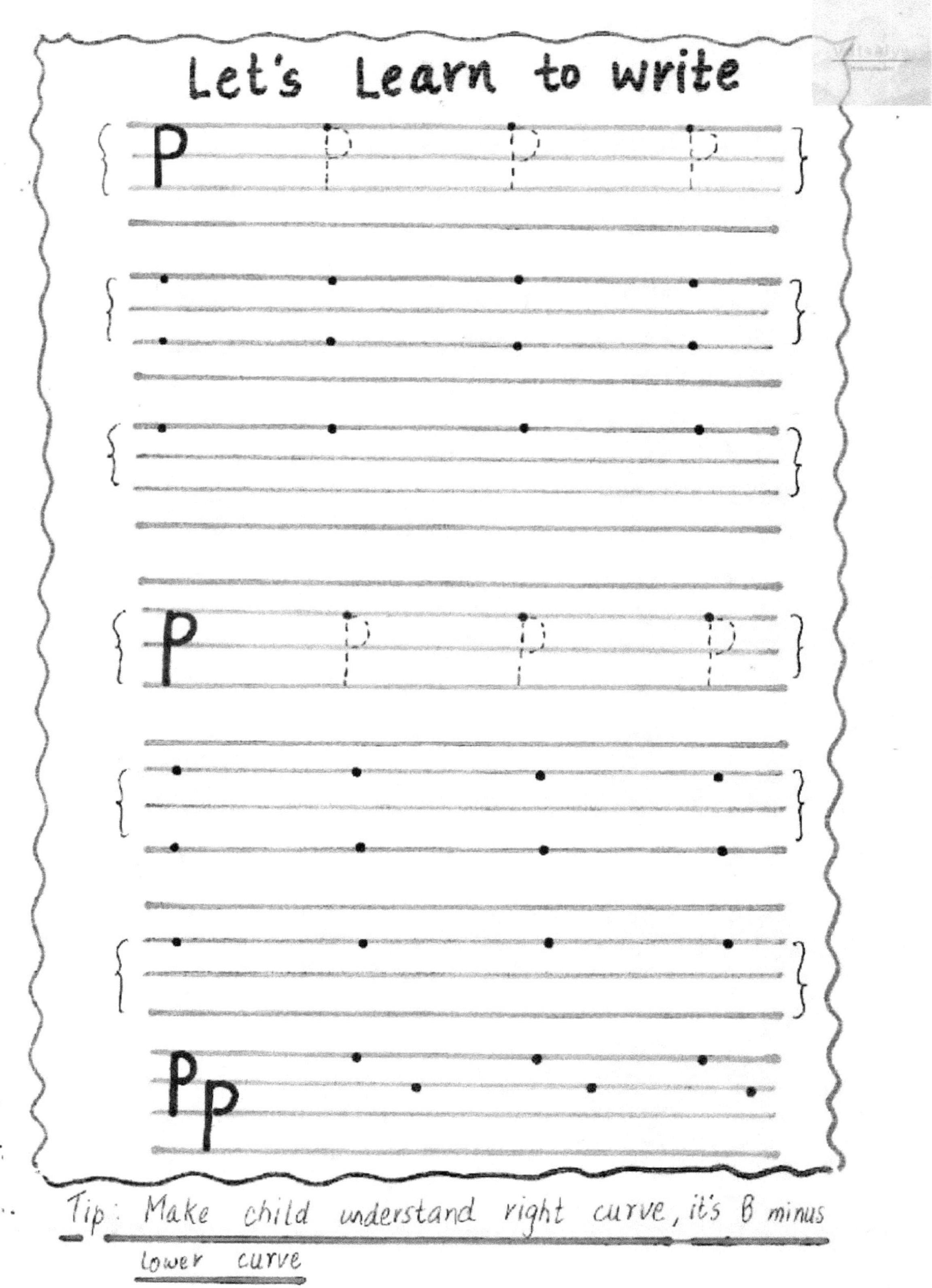

Tip: Make child understand right curve, it's B minus lower curve

52

LETTER Qq

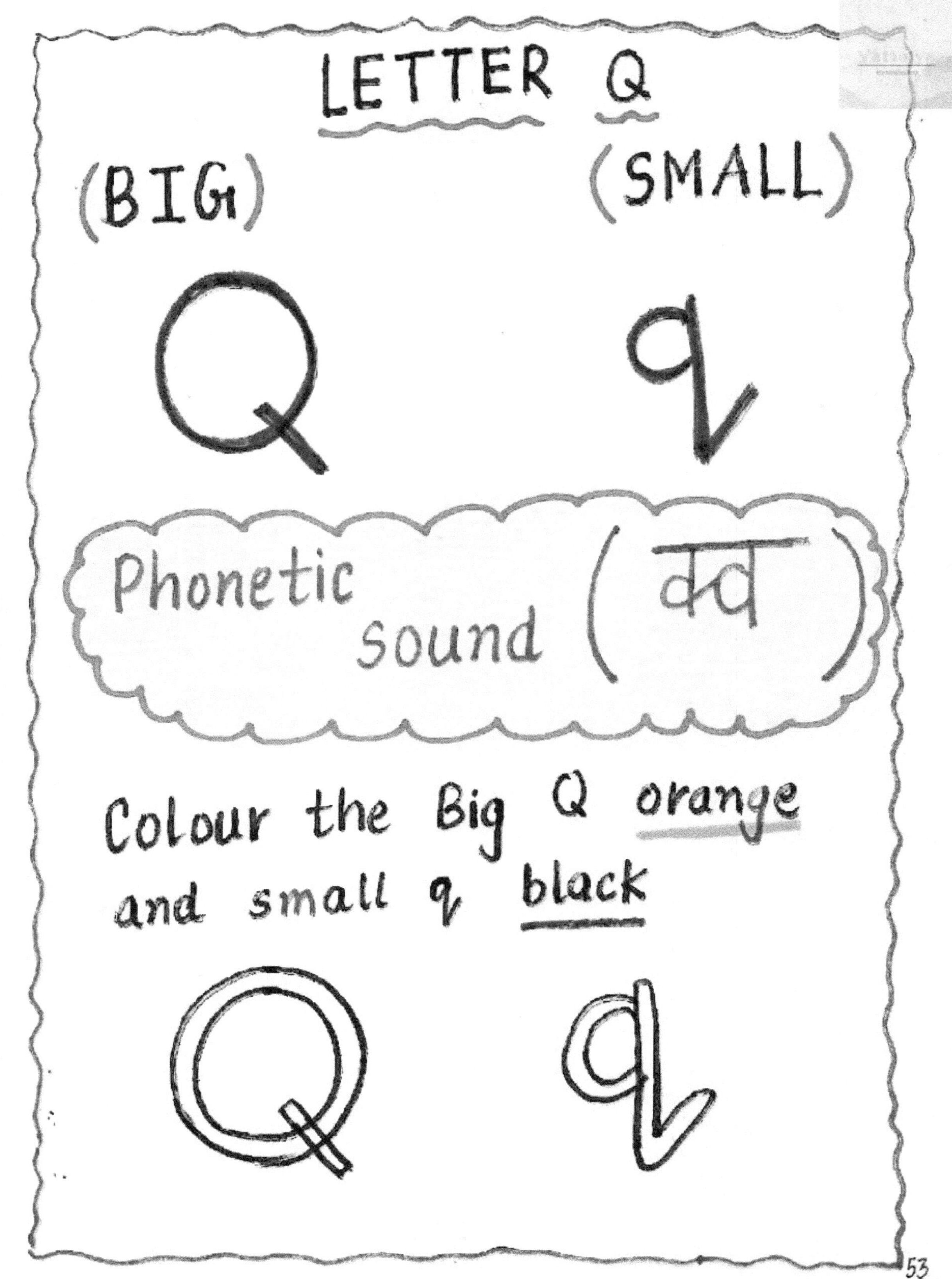
LETTER Q
(BIG)
(SMALL)
Q
q
Phonetic sound (क्व)
Colour the Big Q orange
and small q black
Q
q
53

things with letter
'Q'
(क्व) Quill
(क्व) Question mark
(क्व) Queen
(क्व) Quilt
(क्व) Quarter
(क्व) Quiver
54

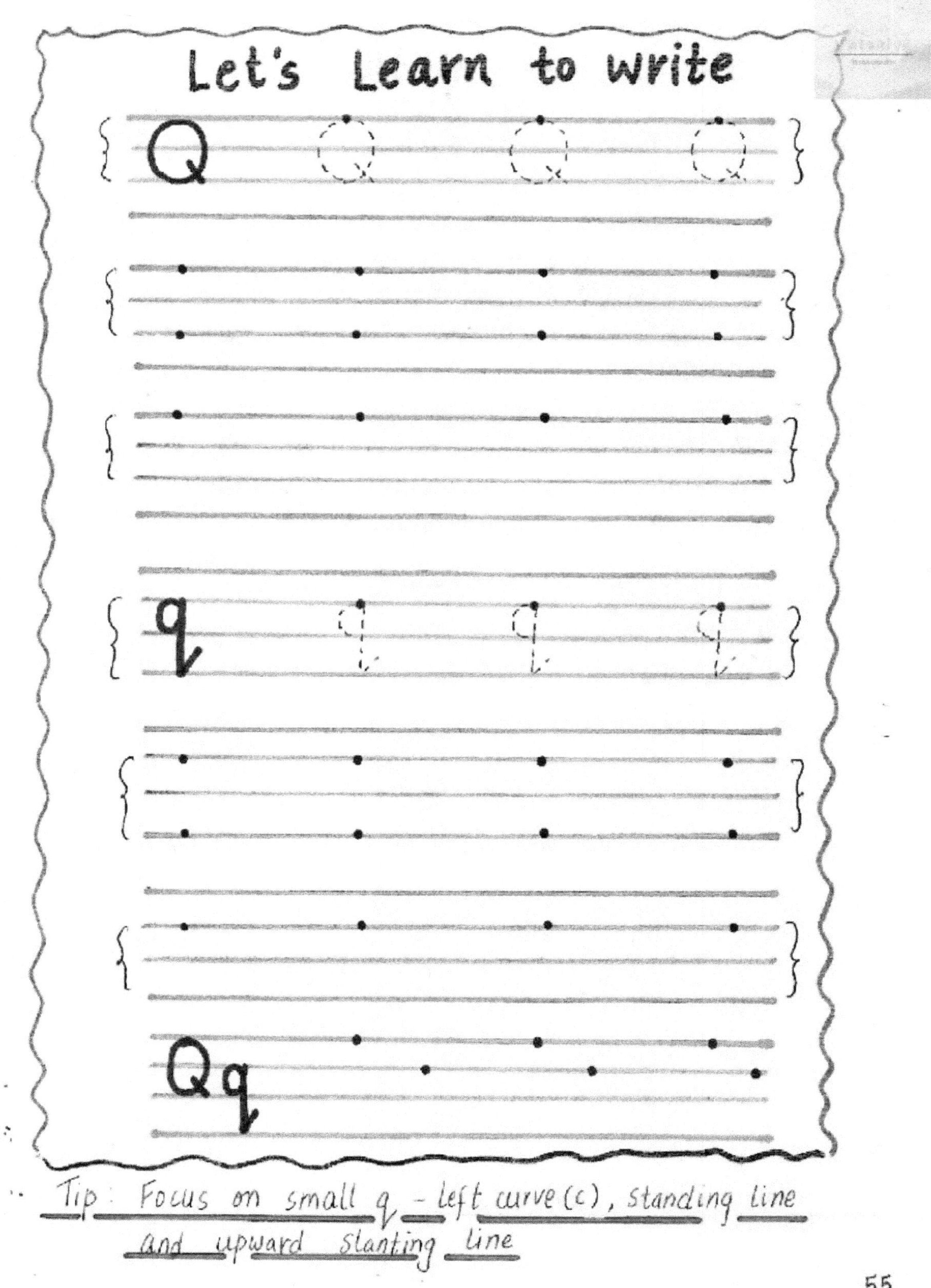

Tip: Focus on small q - left curve (c), standing line and upward slanting line

55

LETTER Rr

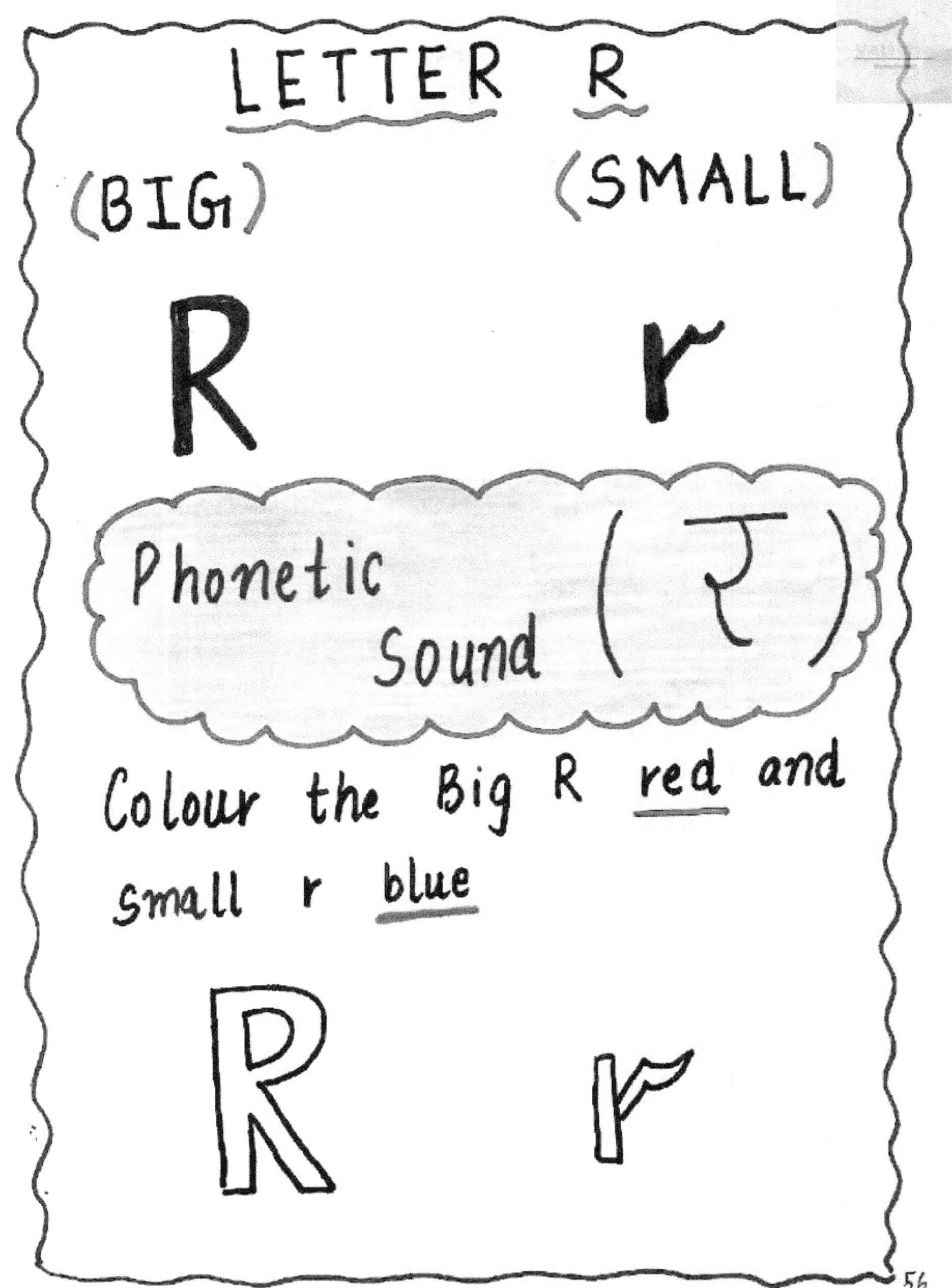

LETTER R R
(BIG)
(SMALL)
R
r
Phonetic Sound (र)
Colour the Big R red and small r blue
R
r
56

things with letter 'R'

(र) Rainbow

(र) Raddish

(र) Rocket

(र) Rose

(र) Ring

(र) Rhino

57

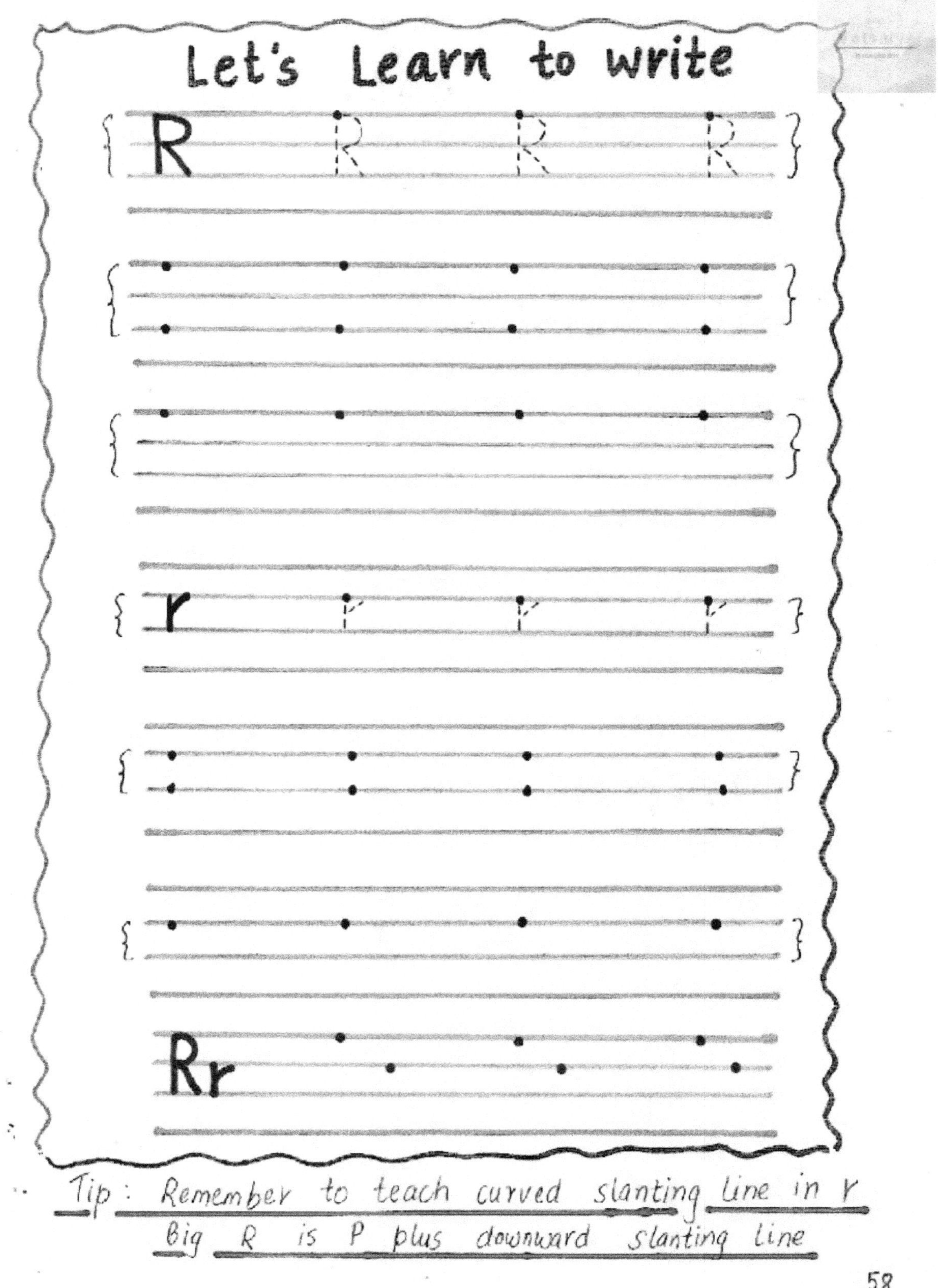

Tip : Remember to teach curved slanting line in r
Big R is P plus downward slanting line

58

LETTER Ss

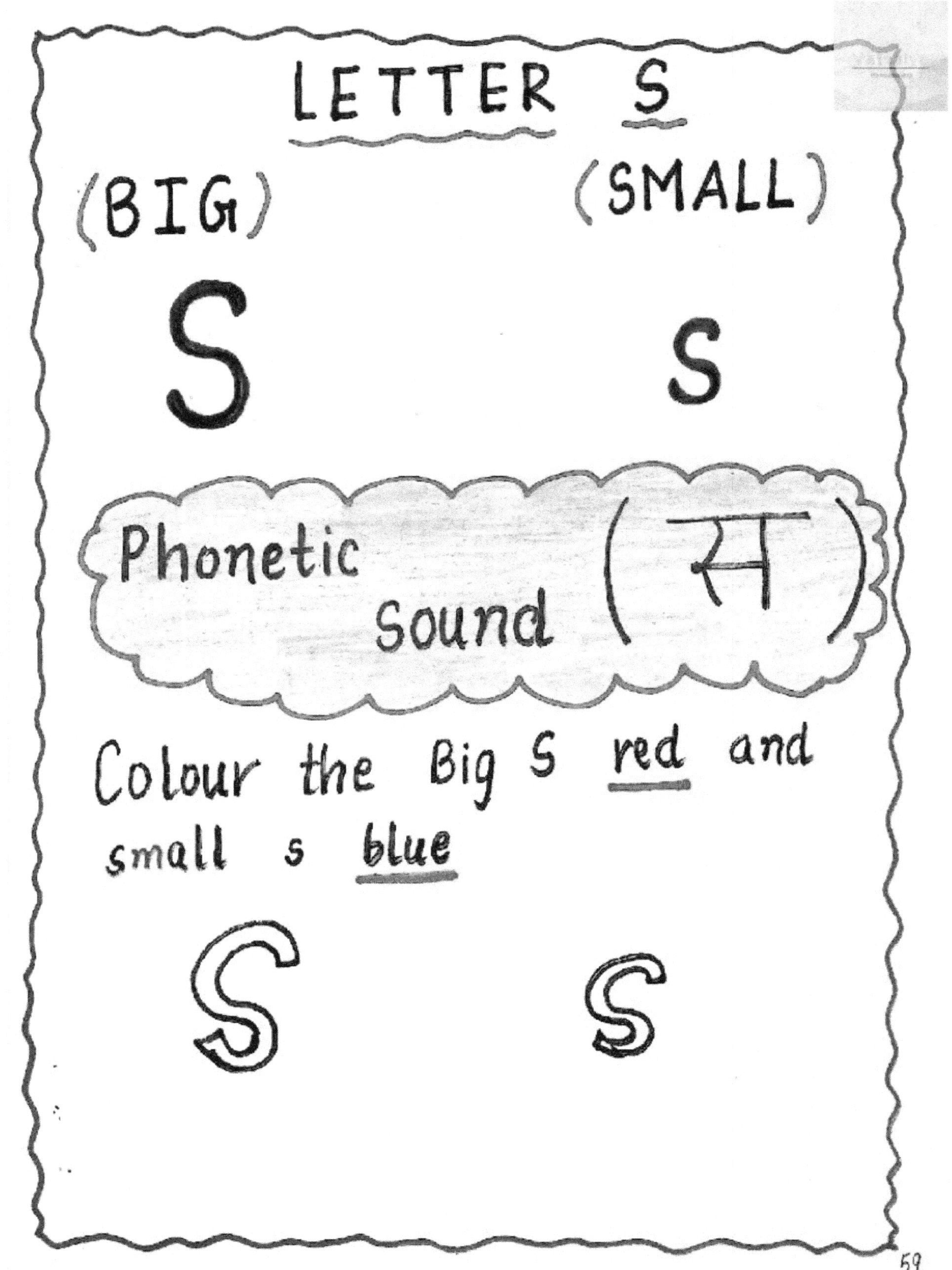

LETTER S
(BIG)
(SMALL)
S
s
Phonetic Sound (स)
Colour the Big S red and small s blue
S
s

things with letter 'S'

(स) Star

(स) Spaceship

(स) Sunflower

(स) Snake

(स) Starfish

(स) Snow man

Let's Learn to write
S S S S
S S S S
S s
Tip: S and s are c and inverted c together
61

LETTER Tt

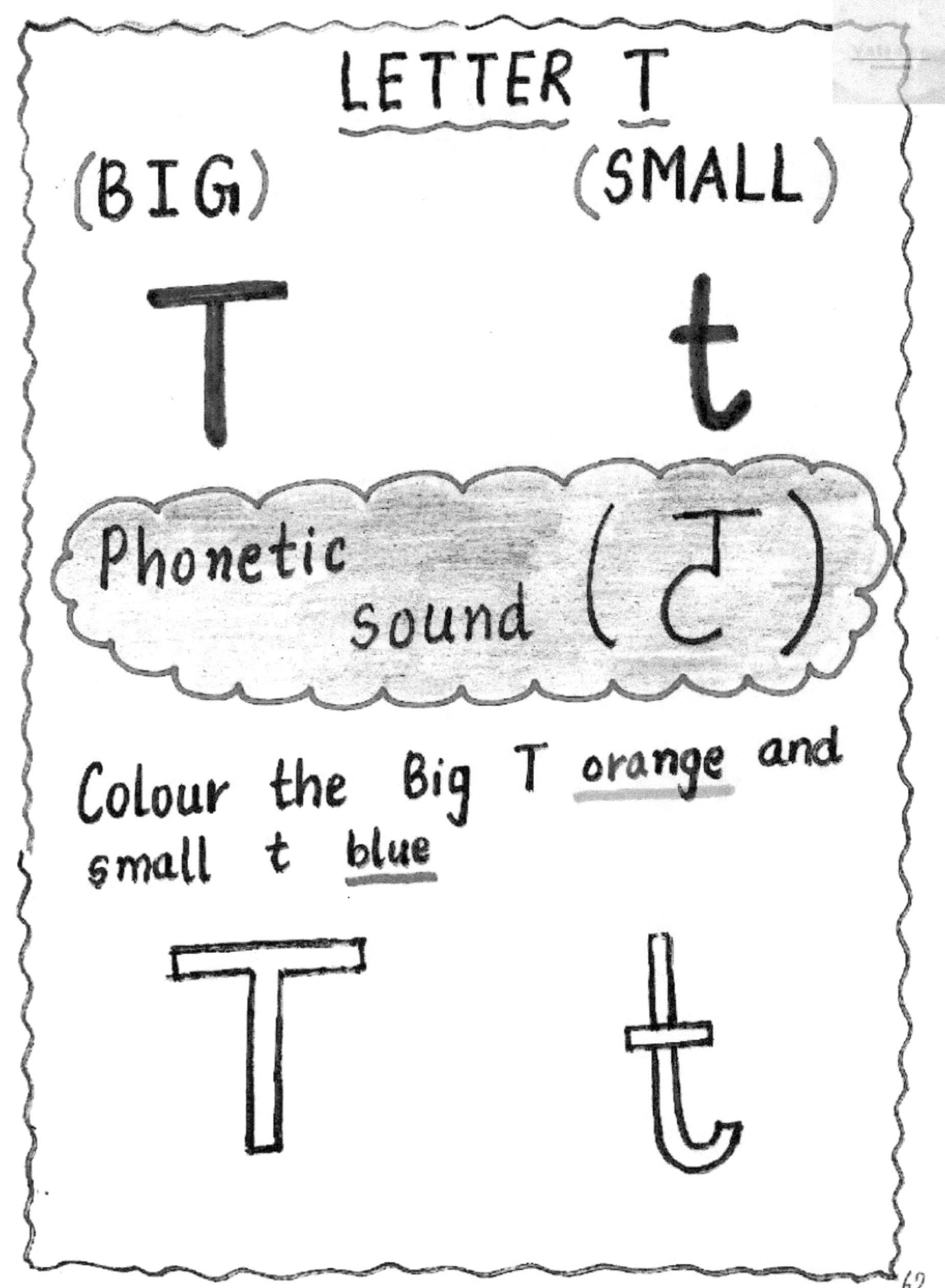

LETTER T
(BIG)
(SMALL)
T
t
Phonetic sound (ट)
Colour the Big T orange and small t blue

62

things with letter 'T'

(ट) Tree

(ट) T-shirt

(ट) Two

(ट) Tooth

(ट) Tulip

(ट) Ten

Let's Learn to write

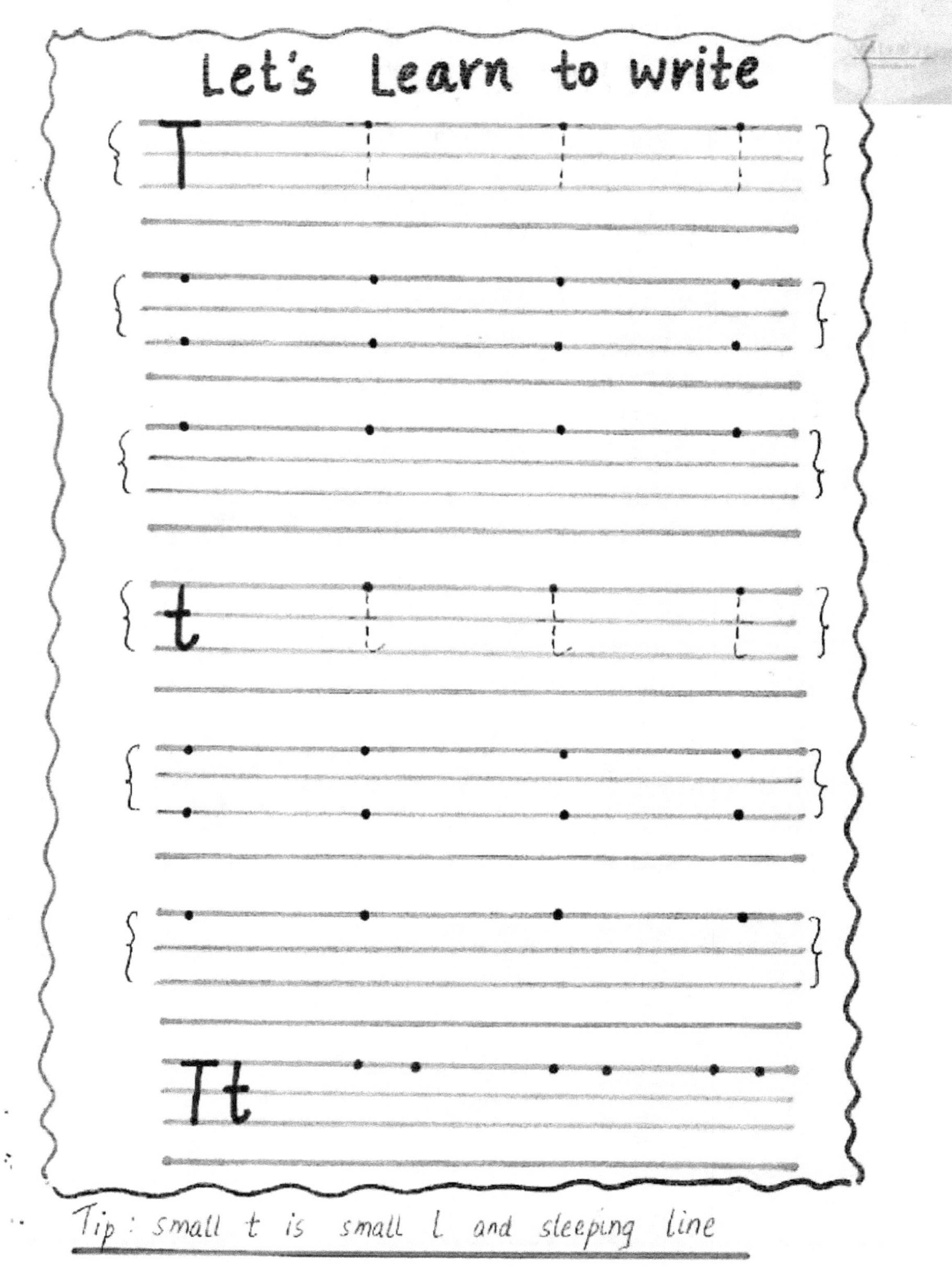

Tip: small t is small l and sleeping line

64

LETTER Uu

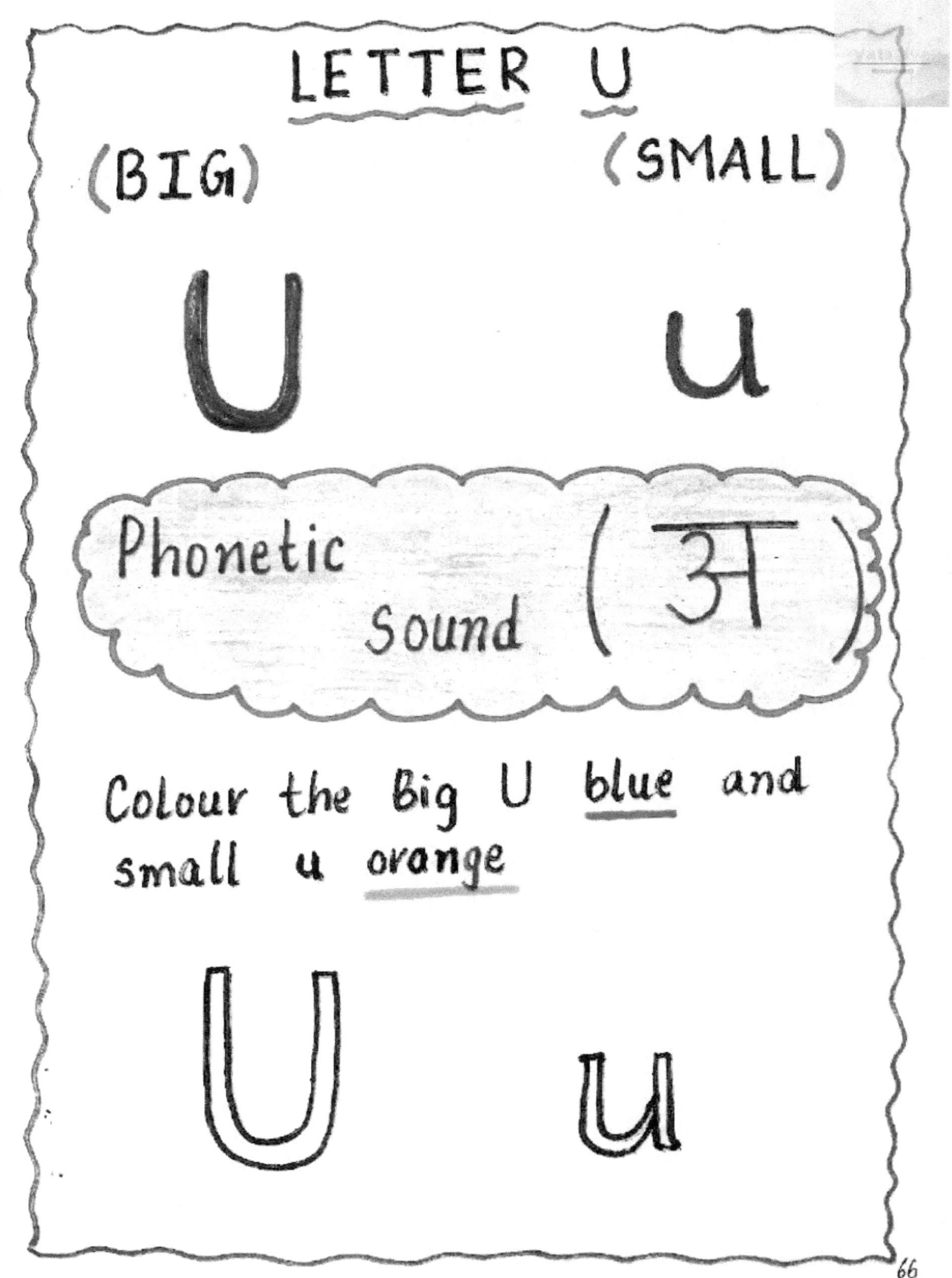

LETTER U
(BIG)
(SMALL)
U
u
Phonetic Sound (अ)
Colour the Big U blue and small u orange
U
u

LETTER U

(BIG)   (SMALL)

U   u

Phonetic Sound (अ)

Colour the Big U _blue_ and small u _orange_

U   u

66

things with letter 'U'

65

LETTER Vv

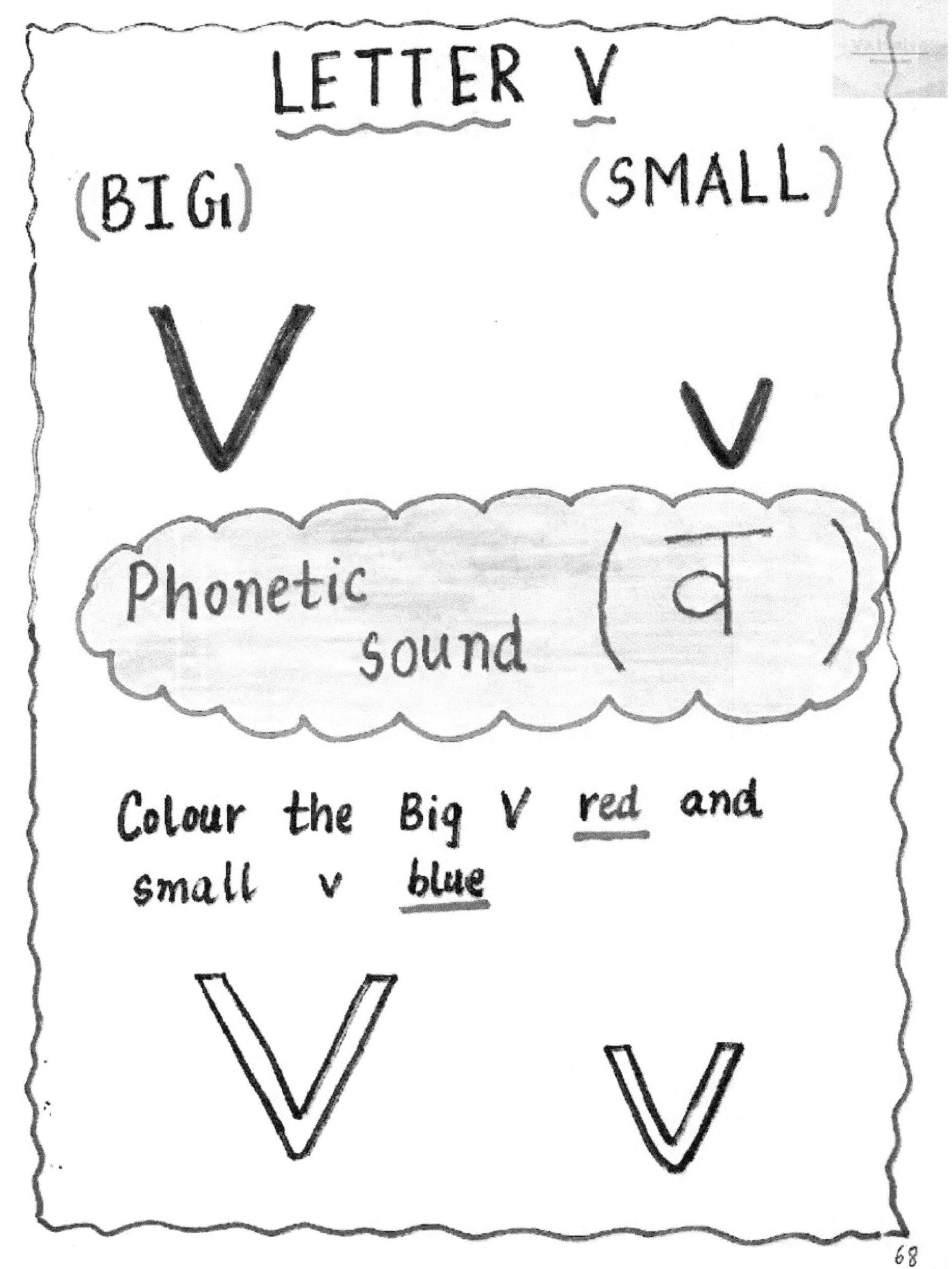

LETTER V
(BIG)
(SMALL)
Phonetic sound (व)
Colour the Big V red and
small v blue
68

things with letter 'V'

69

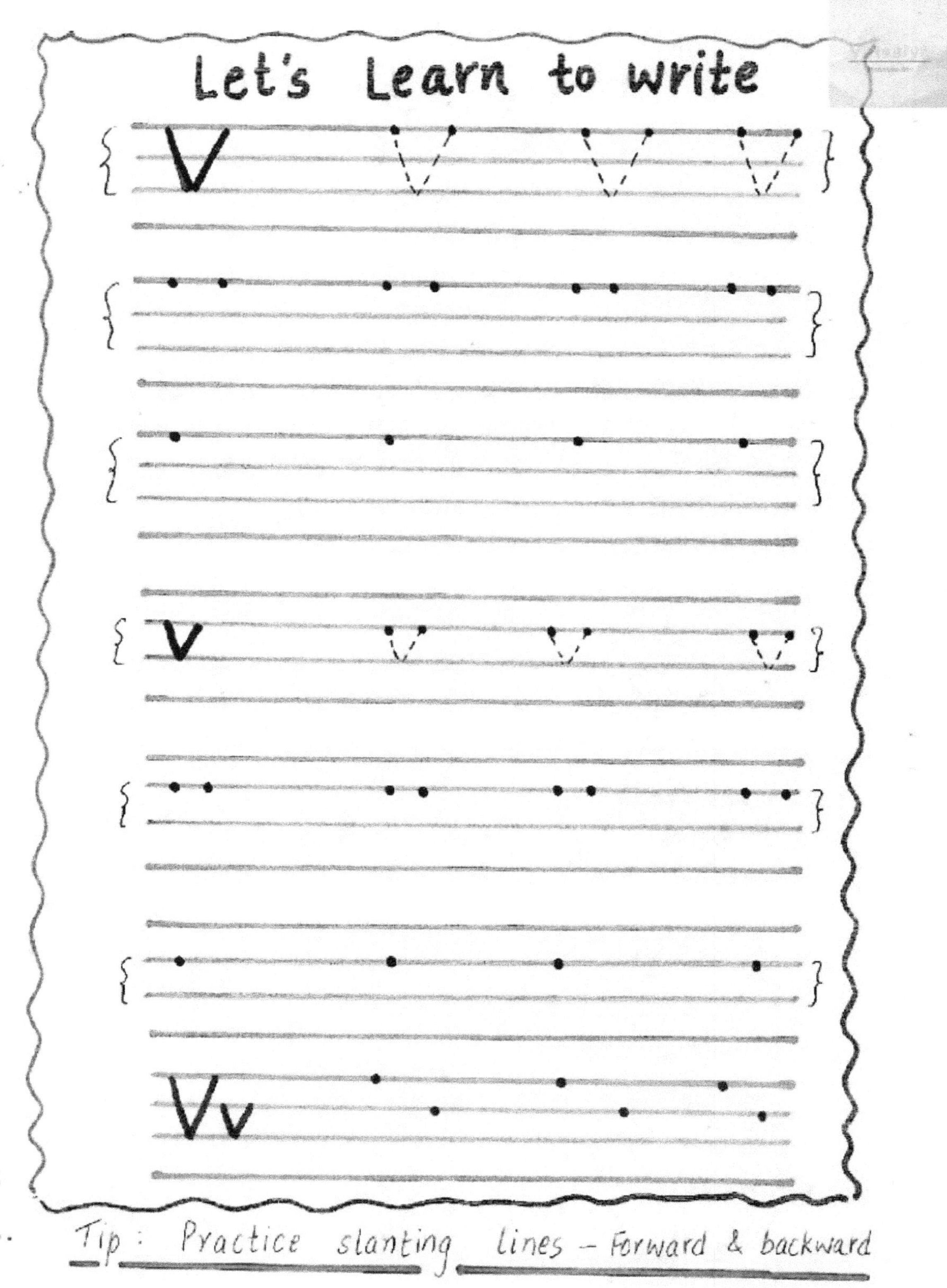

Tip: Practice slanting lines — Forward & backward

70

LETTER Ww

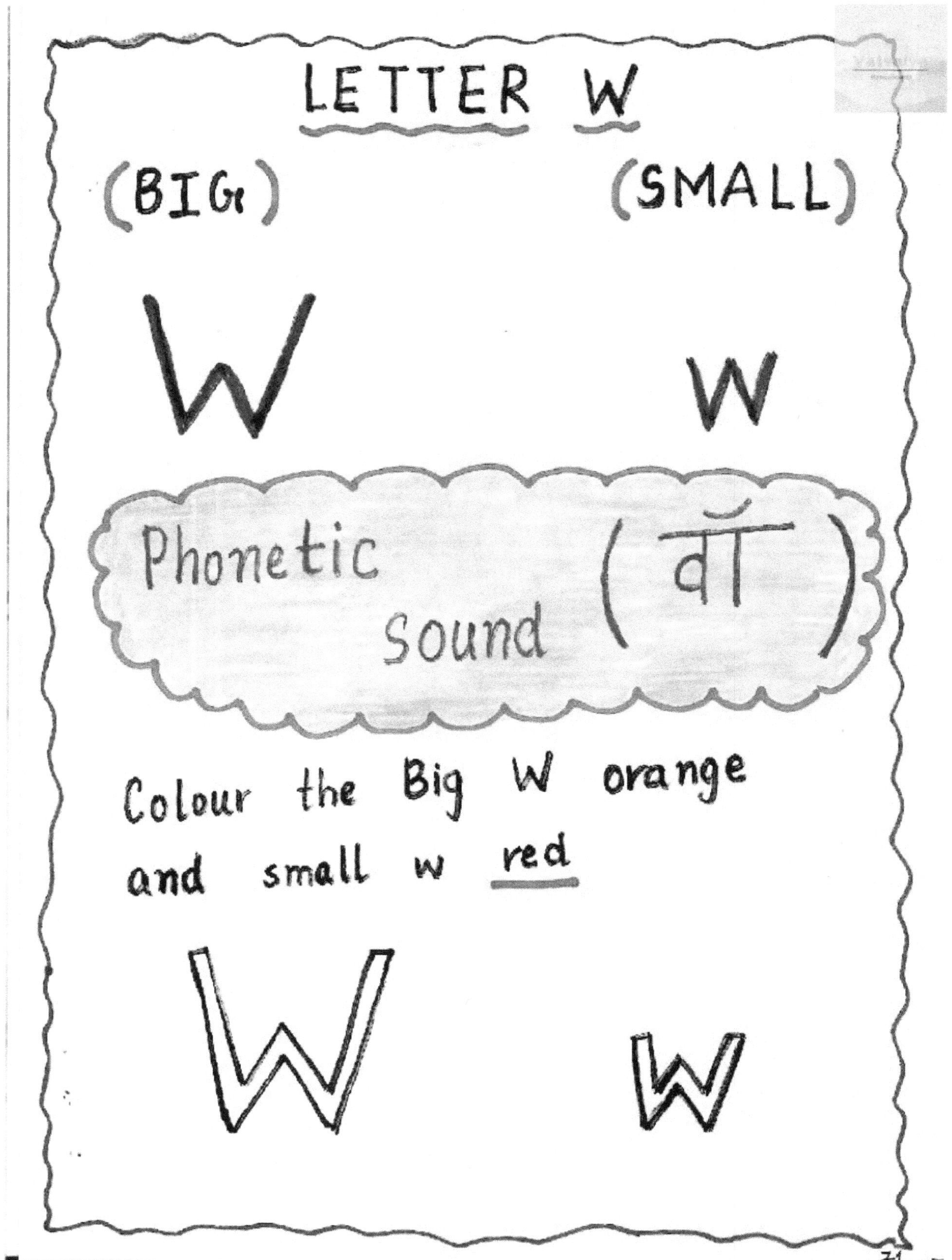

LETTER W
(BIG)
(SMALL)
W
W
Phonetic Sound (वॉ)
Colour the Big W orange
and small w red
W
W
71

things with letter 'W'

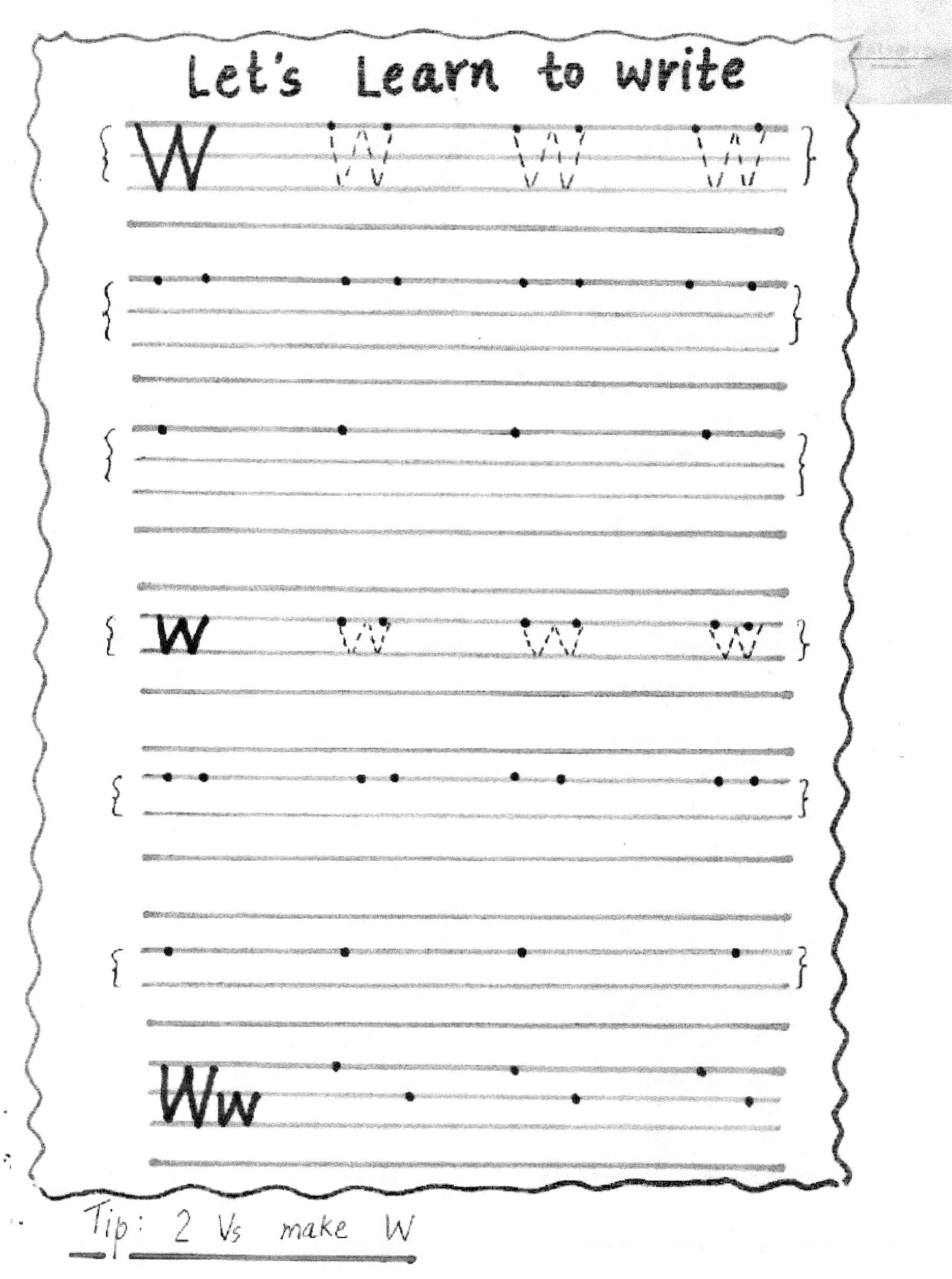

Tip: 2 Vs make W

73

LETTER Xx

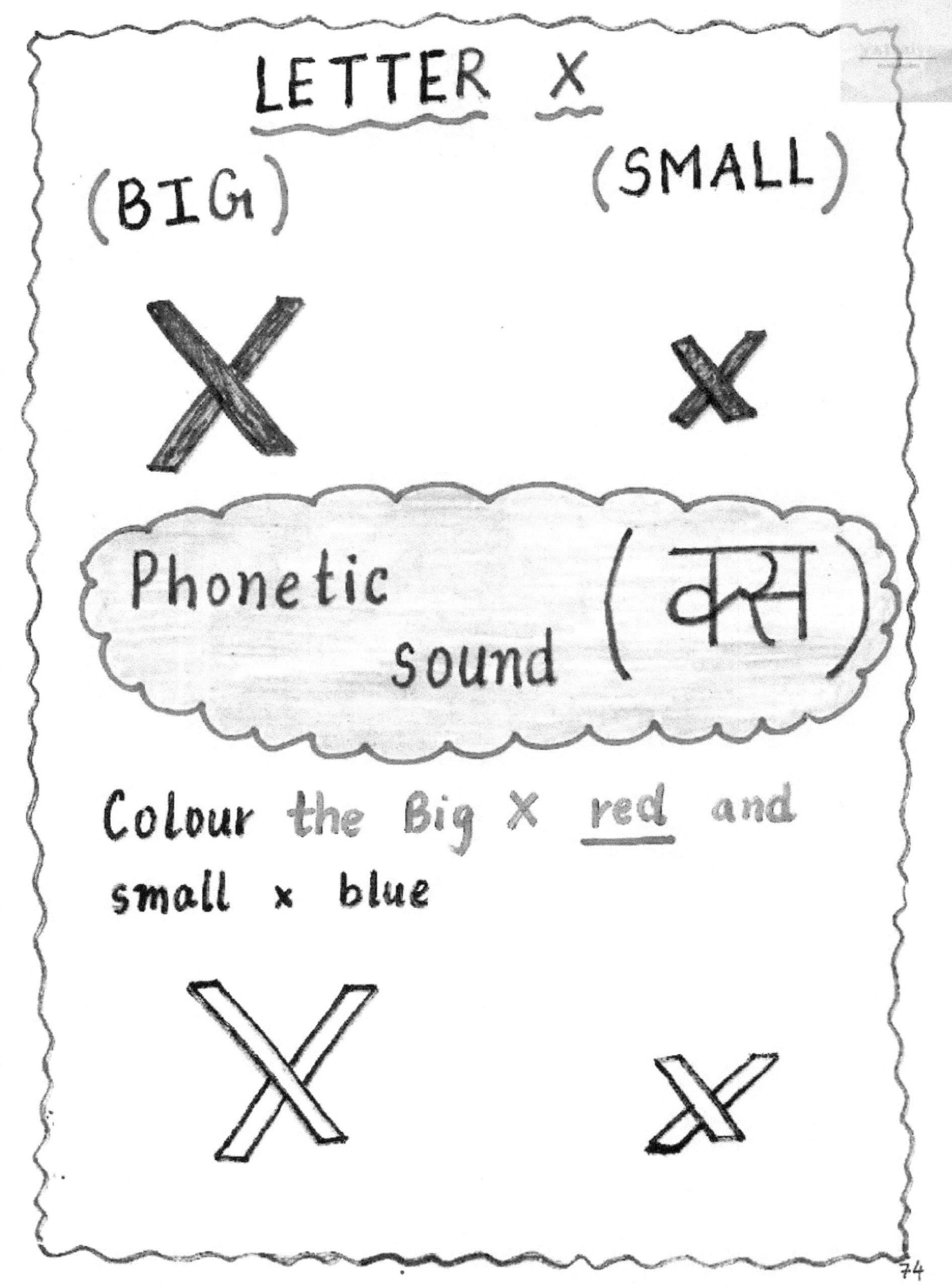

LETTER X
(BIG)
(SMALL)
Phonetic sound (क्स)
Colour the Big X red and small x blue
74

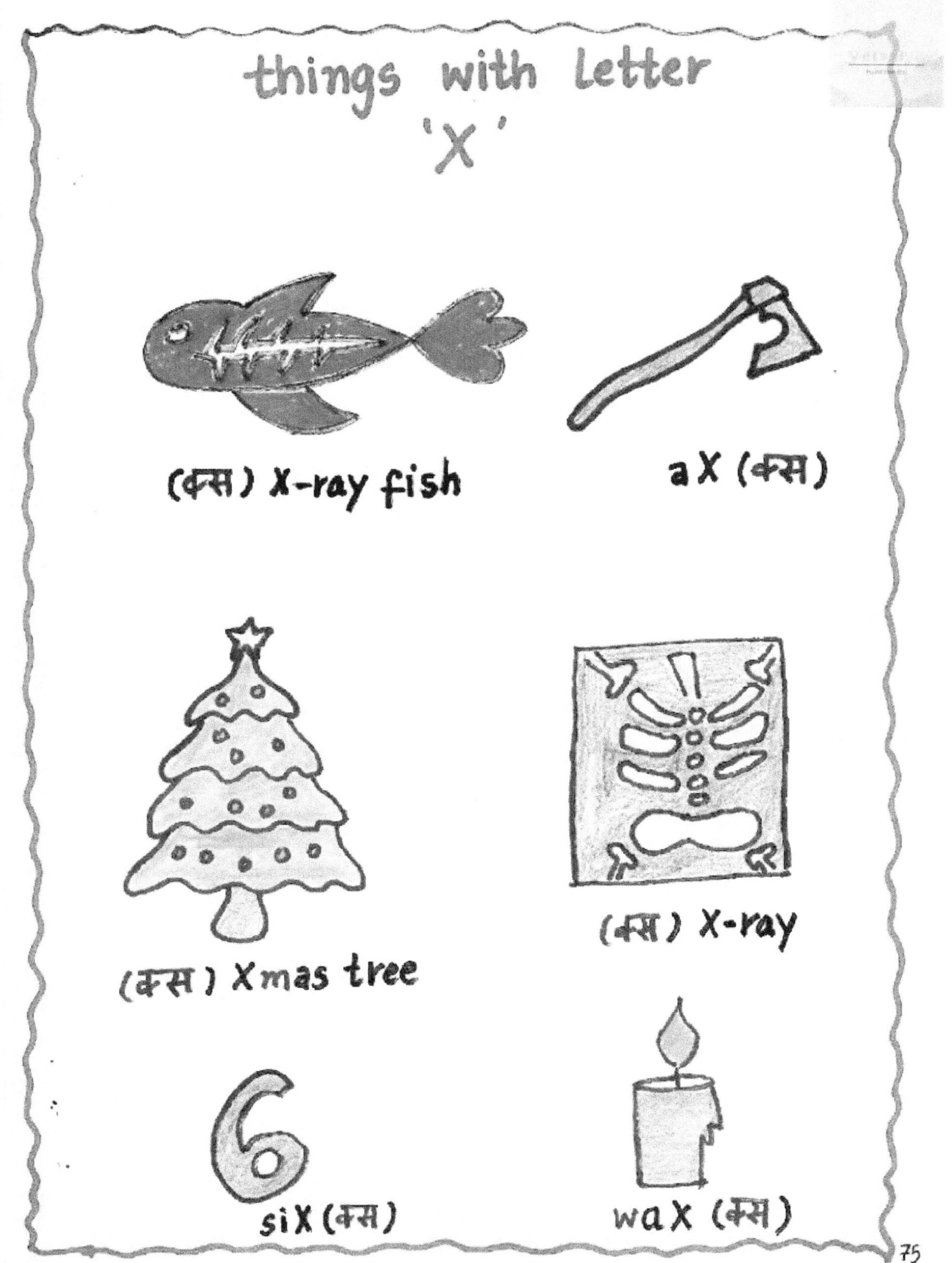

things with letter 'X'
(क्स) X-ray fish
aX (क्स)
(क्स) Xmas tree
(क्स) X-ray
siX (क्स)
waX (क्स)

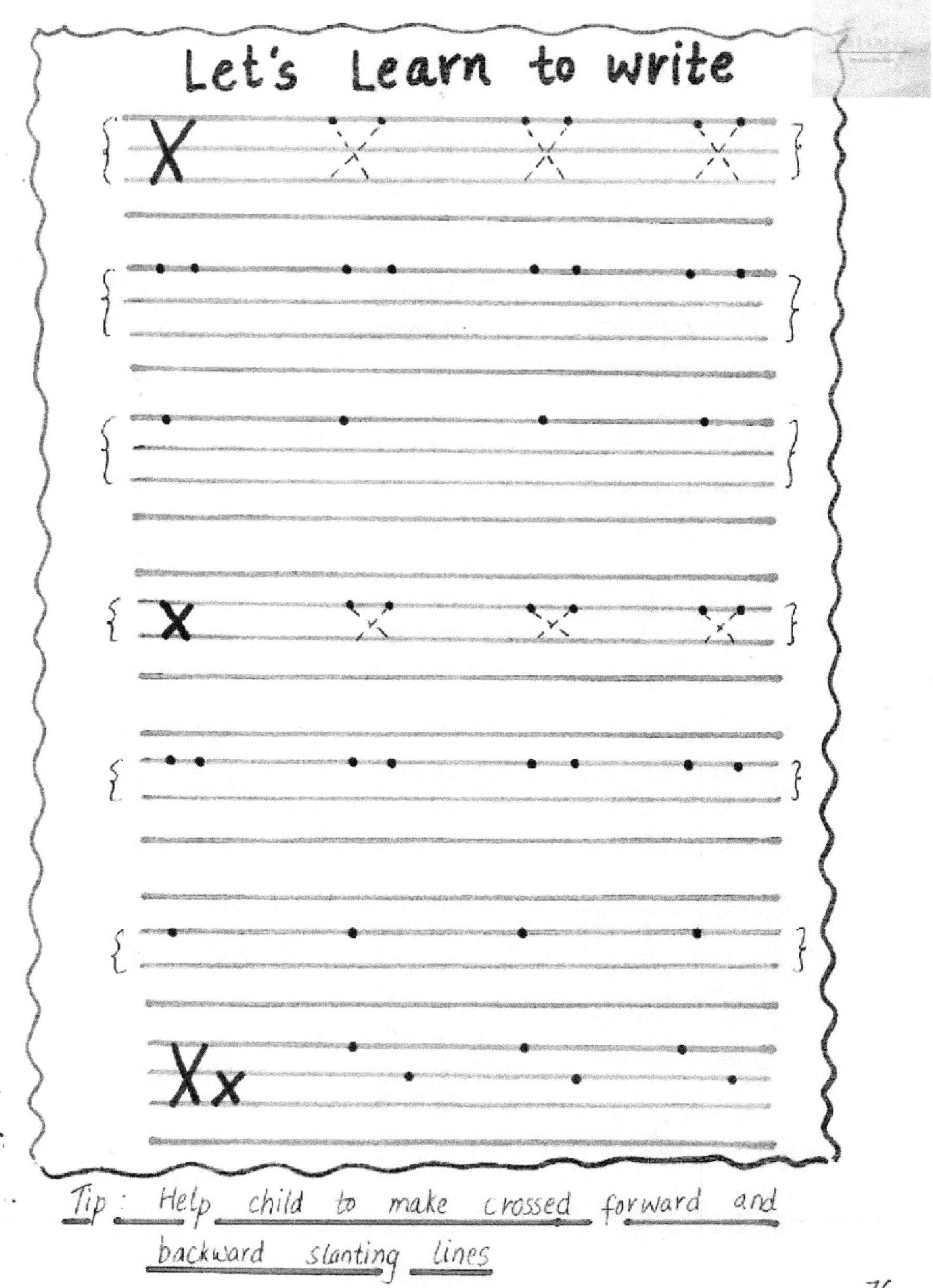

Tip: Help child to make crossed forward and backward slanting lines

76

LETTER Yy

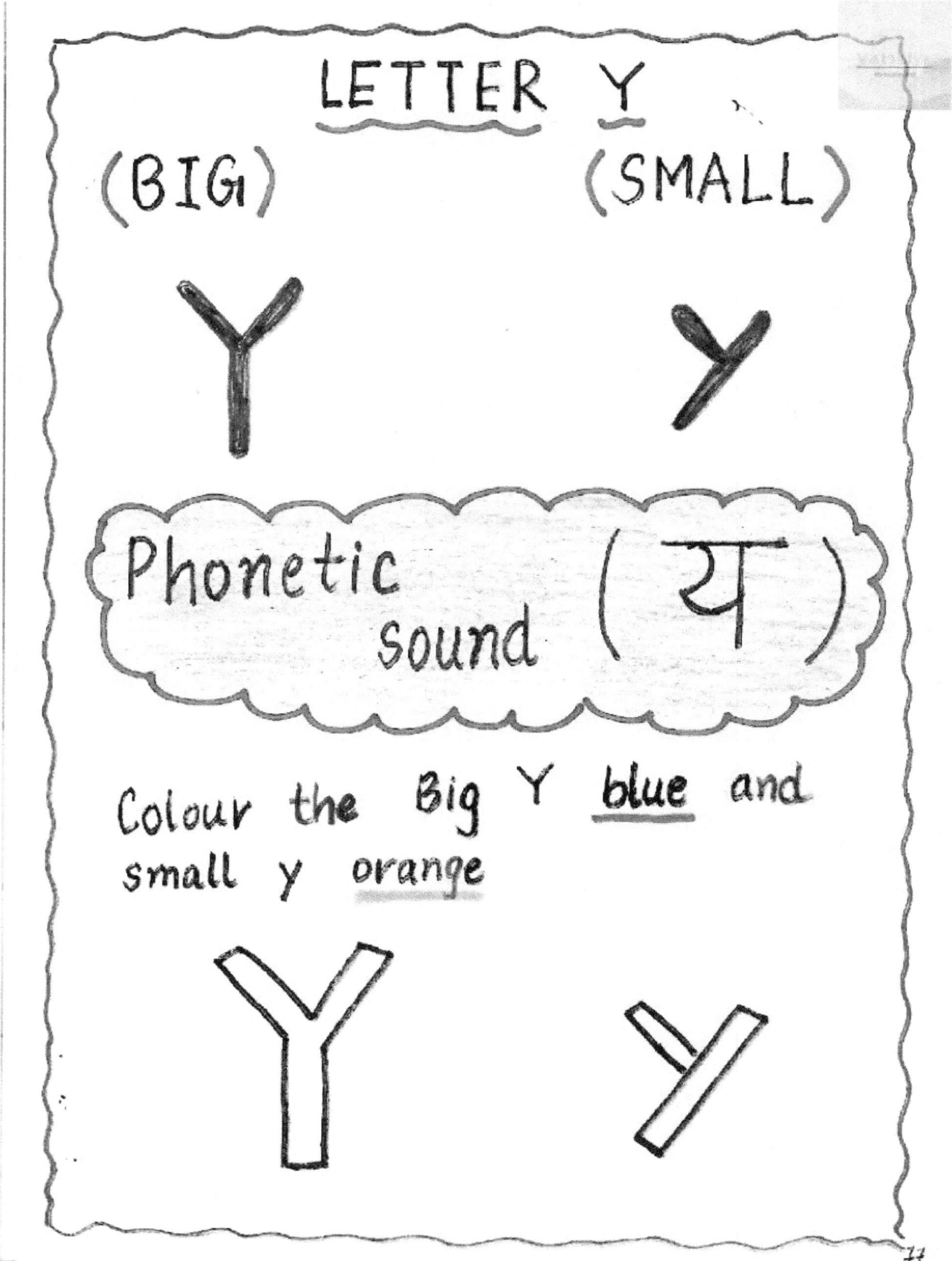

LETTER Y
(BIG)
(SMALL)
Phonetic sound (य)
Colour the Big Y blue and small y orange

things with letter 'Y'

Let's Learn to write

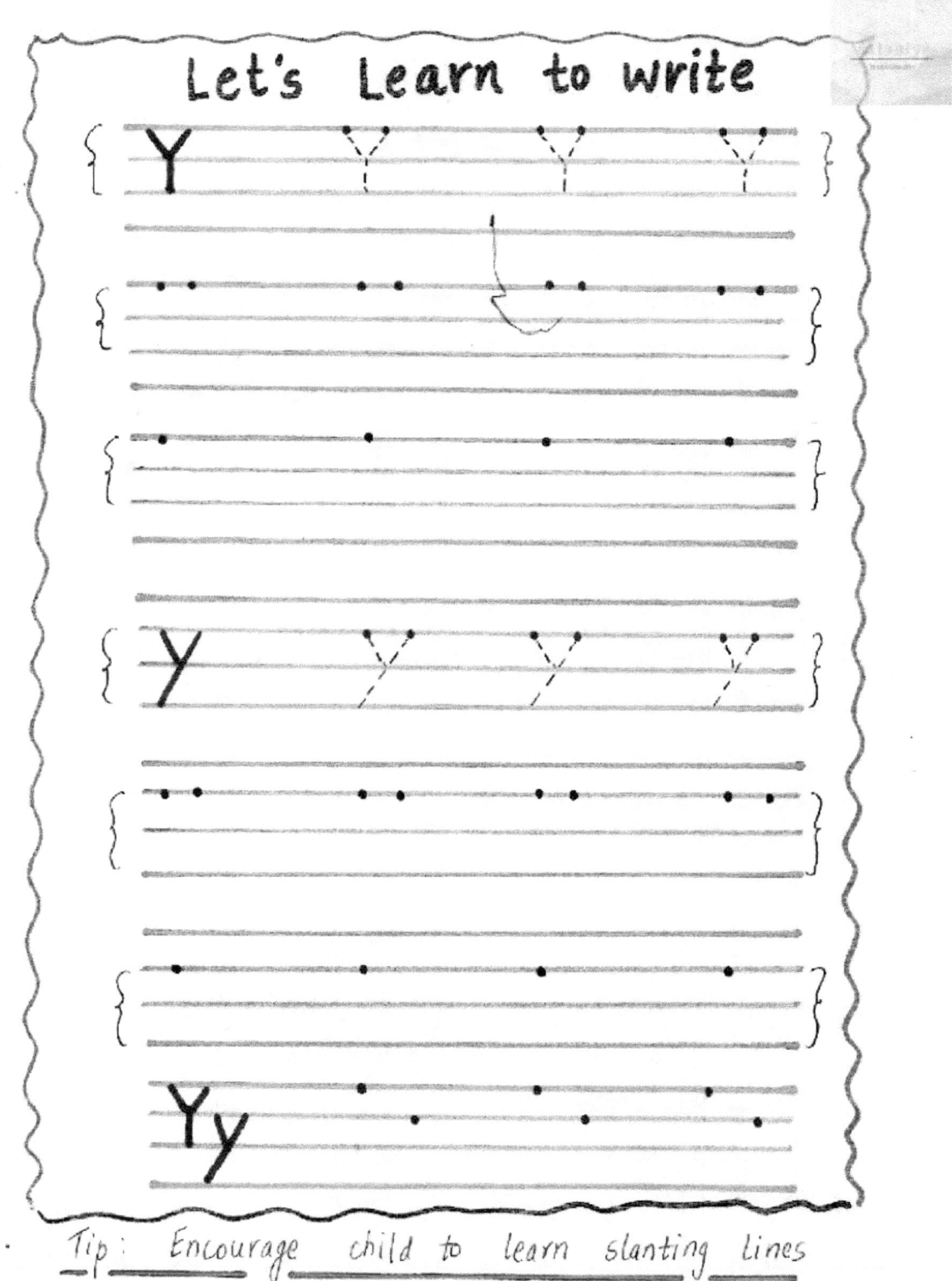

Tip: Encourage child to learn slanting lines

LETTER Zz

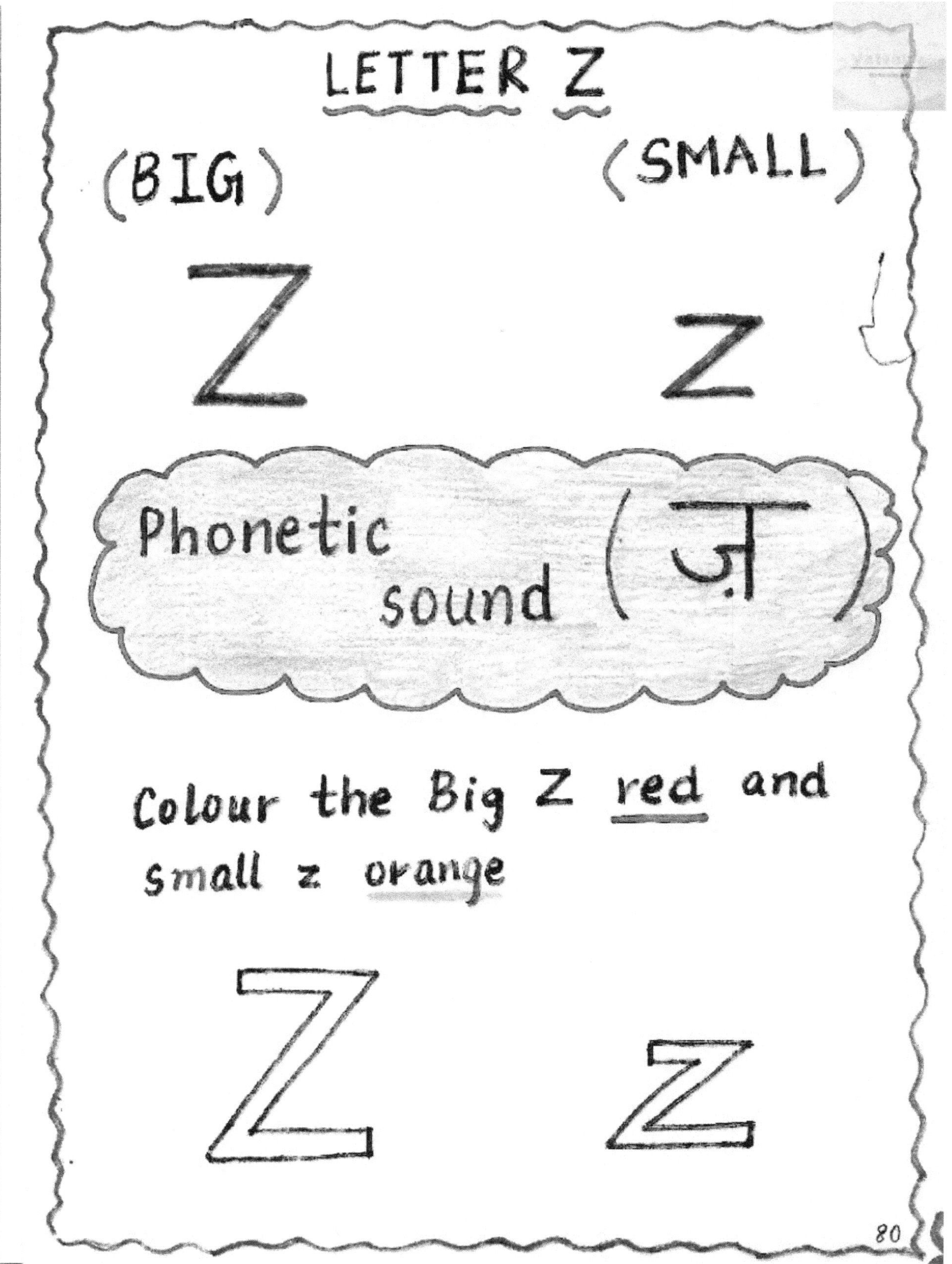
LETTER Z
(BIG)
(SMALL)
Z
z
Phonetic sound (ज़)
Colour the Big Z red and small z orange
Z
z

80

things with letter 'Z'

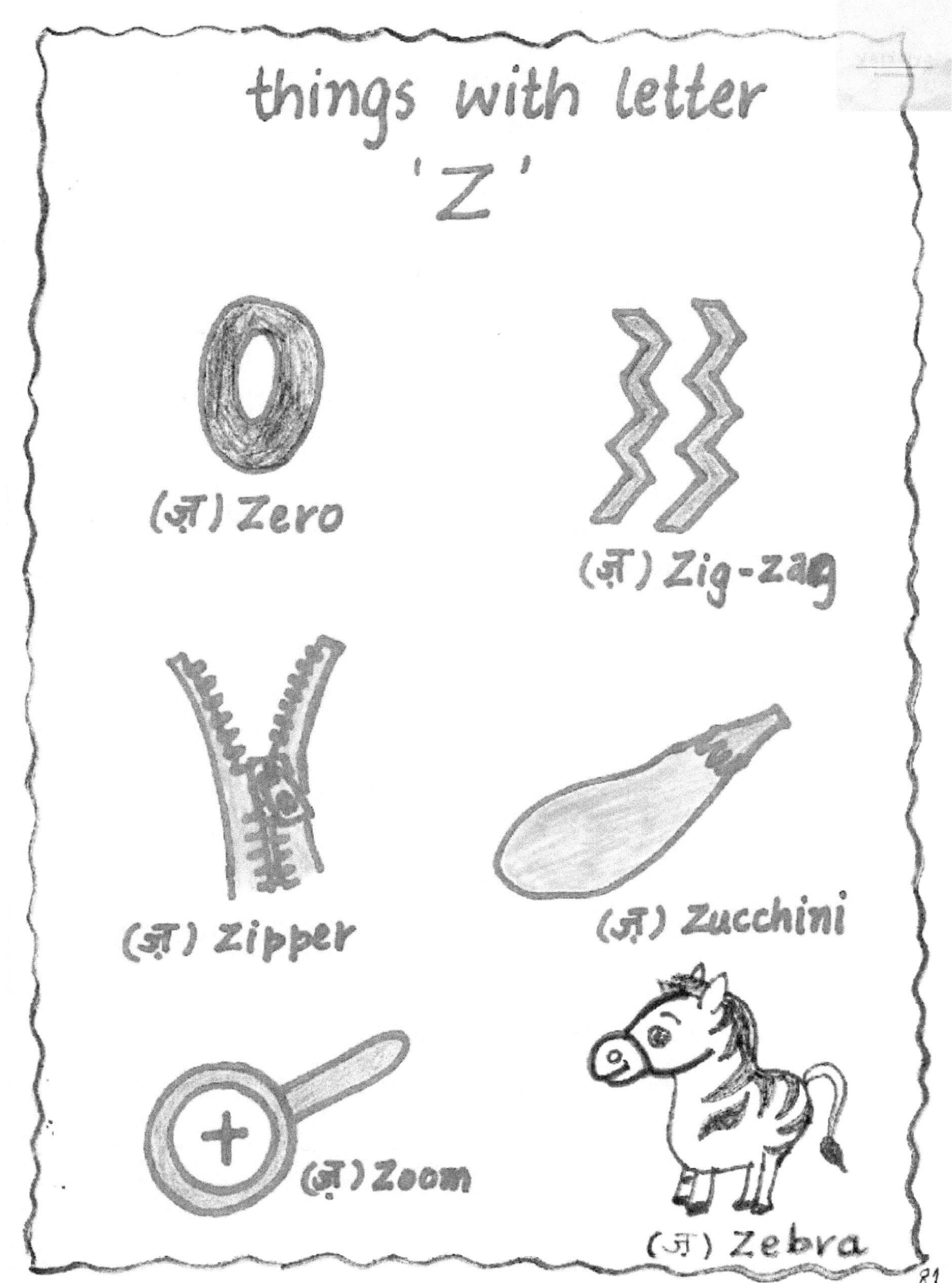

Let's Learn to write

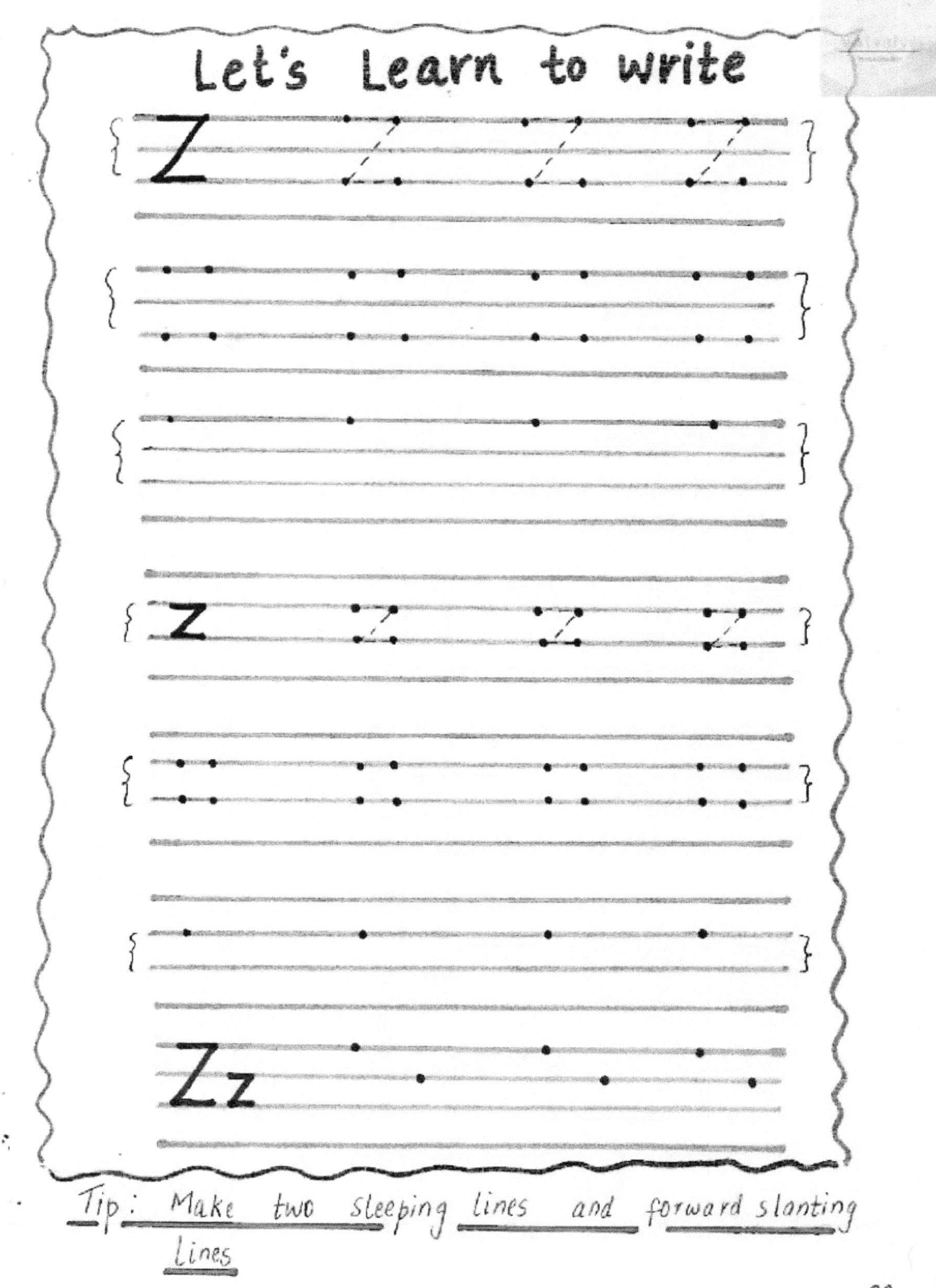

Tip: Make two sleeping lines and forward slanting lines

82

CHAPTER TWENTY-NINE

PRACTICE SHEETS LET US PRACTICE WHAT WE HAVE LEARNT SO FAR!!

Do i remember?
Colour all the circles with Big letters:
I
c
C
U
E
s
b
a
e
q
Q
I
A
t
T
P
B
Z
S
W
V
K
D
x
f
A
L
j
p
O
M
Colour the duckie

Revision of Big & small

Read the letters with their respective sounds. Colour the square with the correct small letter for the given Big letters.

A says ऐ	c	a	e
O says ओ	o	e	c
B says ब	h	d	b
C says स,क	o	c	a
D says ड	d	b	h
E says ए	a	e	o
F says फ	g	f	q
G says ग	q	g	f

85

Phonic based learning

Match the Big and small letters to the correct phonetic sound:

A	ह	h
E	य	a
H	ल	e
Y	ऐ	b
L	ब	l
B	ए	y

Tip: Encourage child to say words with given letters

86

Write the small letter for the given Big letters and then match with the correct picture :
F
T
G
H
B
M
V
87

picture recognition
Help the child identify the pictures.
Now, with the help of phonetic sounds
ask them to colour the correct first letter
a u o
c z i
f b d
b h f
h g q
g q p
a o e
t i r
n o t

DO I REMEMBER ?

Write the suitable letter after identifying the picture :

90

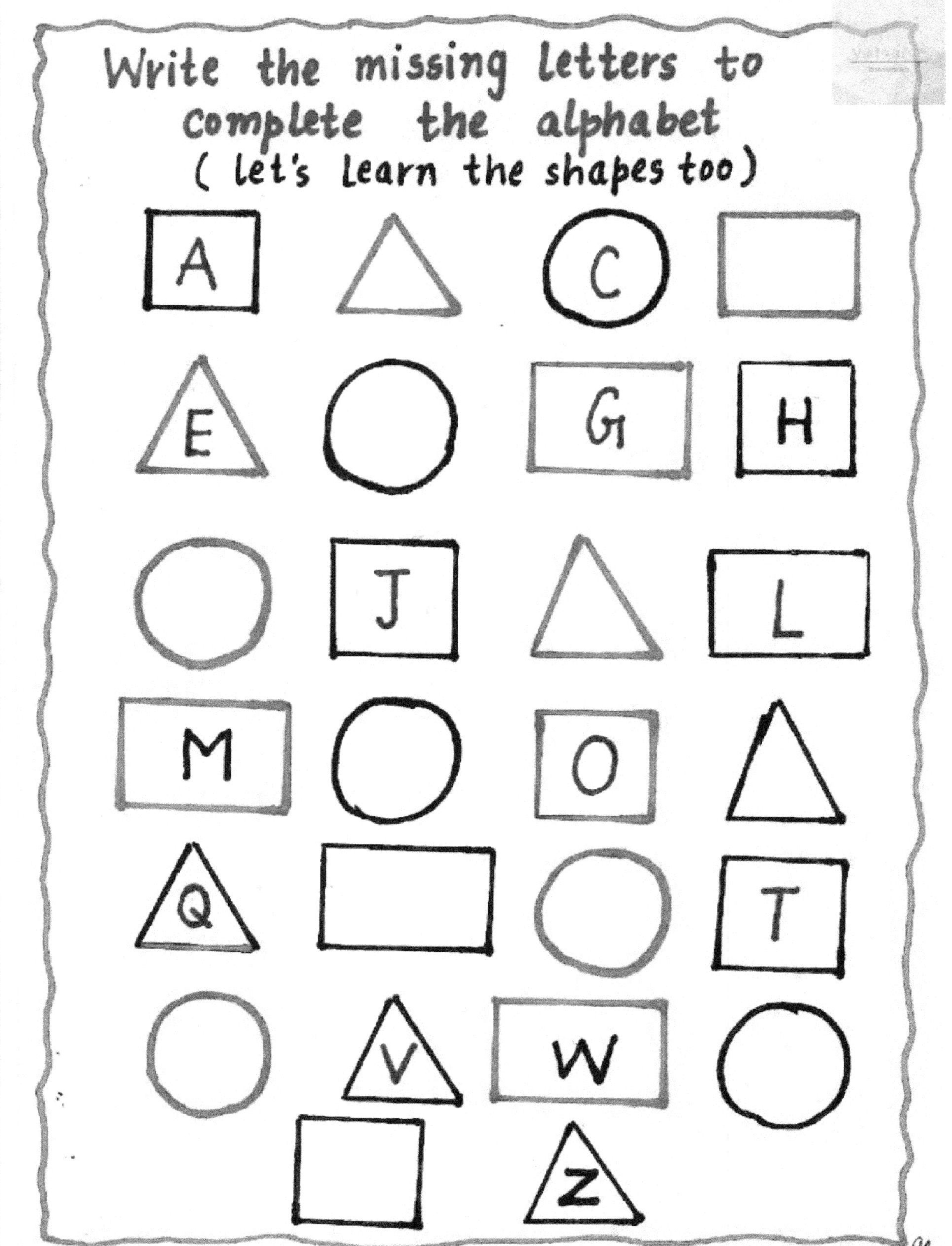

Write the missing letters to complete the alphabet
(let's learn the shapes too)
A
C
E
G
H
J
L
M
O
Q
T
V
W
Z

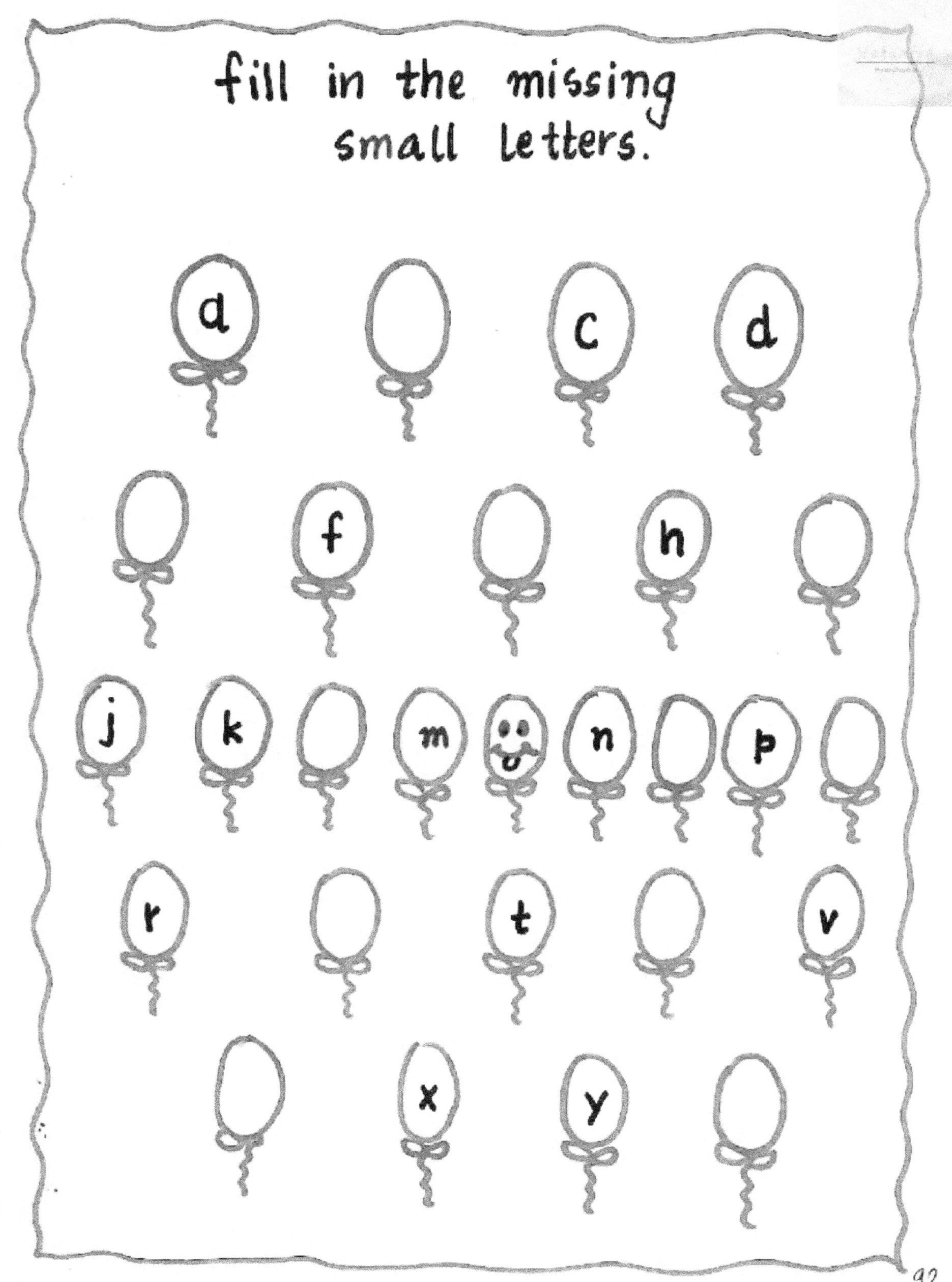

fill in the missing
small letters.
d
c
d
f
h
j
k
m
n
p
r
t
v
x
y

Circle the correct letter for the pictures below :

(Tip: Help child memorise the phonetic sounds)

(ब) Book

h b d

(ल) Lips

t l k

(ह) Hat

b d h

(क) Kite

k l m

(क्व) Question

c k q

93

Identify the national animal
of India by joining the
dots from A to Z

(Colour the
animal)

Hello, I am _ IGER !

94

Write the Big letters for the given small letters. Colour the picture which represents the letters.
p
q
r
s
t
SOAP
95

Identify the picture and write the corresponding Big & small letters (tip: focus on given sounds)
अ
व
वाँ
क्स
य
ज़

Let's Learn to write
A a
Z z

Let's Learn to write

98

Let's Learn to write

THREE LETTER WORDS

three letter words

Encourage child to read three letter words by joining sounds. Let's see how!

JAR	ज + ऐ + र	जार
FUN	फ + अ + न	फन
HUT	ह + अ + ट	हट
PEN	प + ए + न	पेन
CAT	क + ऐ + ट	कैट
BIB	ब + इ + ब	बिब
LEG	ल + ए + ग	लेग
FOX	फ + ओ + क्स	फोक्स
FAN	फ + ऐ + न	फैन

Many more three letter words can be practiced in a similar manner.

100

CHAPTER THIRTY-ONE

CHECKLIST

Checklist

Letter recognition		Phonetic sound	Vocabulary
A	a		
B	b		
C	c		
D	d		
E	e		
F	f		
G	g		
H	h		
I	i		
J	j		
K	k		
L	l		
M	m		
N	n		
O	o		
P	p		
Q	q		
R	r		
S	s		
T	t		
U	u		
V	v		
W	w		
X	x		
Y	y		
Z	z		

Educator at the end of completion, tick the milestones

101

Thank You!

HOPE THE EDUCATORS FIND THIS BOOK USEFUL. PLEASE GIVE FEEDBACK ON THE BOOK. IT WILL HELP ME TO IMPROVE IN THE UPCOMING PARTS OF THIS HOMESCHOOLING KIT.